Discovering
Community

A Meditation on

Community

in Christ

Stephen V. Doughty

UPPER
ROOM BOOKS
NASHVILLE

The Upper Room Web Site: http://www.upperroom.org

Cover design: Jim McAnally
Cover illustration: Rebecca Ruegger
First printing: 1999

Library of Congress Cataloging-in-Publication

Doughty, Stephen V.
    Discovering community: a meditation on community in Christ / Stephen V. Doughty.
        p.   cm.
    Includes bibliographical references.
    ISBN 0-8358-0870-X
    1. Church—Meditations 2. Community—Religious aspects—Christianity—Meditations I. Title.
BV600.2.D66   1999   98-20639
262—dc21   CIP

Printed in the United States of America

For

Betty and Bill Doughty
Til and Charlie Fontaine

with love

Contents

Acknowledgments

I WISH TO express my thanks to the laity, pastors, and congregations of Lake Michigan Presbytery for all that they have taught me of community in Christ in recent years and for their steady encouragement to take time for reflecting together on the life we share. Similarly I would thank each congregation that received and nurtured me through the years of pastoral ministry: in the Saint Lawrence River Valley, the Scotch Presbyterian Church of Chipman Corners and the First Presbyterian Church of Waddington, New York; in the Black Hills, the First Presbyterian Church of Lead, South Dakota; in Pennsylvania, the six congregations of the Northwest Area Ministry, these being the Presbyterian churches of Cherry Run, Curllsville, Fisher, Hawthorn and Miola, and the United Church of Christ at Alcola. For their honest speaking, their presence, and their steady care, I owe them more than I can return. I also would offer my thanks to the Shalem Institute for Spiritual Formation and to the particular community of friends from that body who have offered their quietness and their prayers for nearly a decade now: Sister Marie Grace Blum, Father Don Dilg, Gretchen and Keith

Kingsley, Delcy Kuhlman, Shirley Souder and Doris Strife. I am immensely grateful to John Mogabgab, Marjorie J. Thompson, and George Donigian of The Upper Room, each of whom has offered encouragement for these explorations. I want to thank Rita Collett for her thoughtful and caring work with the manuscript. I express my deepest thanks to my wife, Jean, for her patience, her love, and her ever-present sense of fun!

An Experiment
and Beckonings...

THIS SMALL book is the product of an experiment and a series of beckonings. The experiment came first. It arose one Sunday afternoon and, as I defined it, was utterly simple. For one hour near the end of each week I would write whatever came to mind in response to the question, "Where this past week have I actually seen Christian community?" Arbitrarily I decided I would continue this practice for four months and then stop. That would be it. Nothing more.

The experiment was, I must admit, environmentally prodded. Winter, which annually thrills me for six weeks, had been around long enough. Snow now slid from the trees rather than glistened. It matted and clumped along the sidewalks. The brilliance of an exceptionally gorgeous fall was little more than a dull memory and the prospect of spring had, as yet, produced no shoots of hope in my mind.

On a more immediate level, another matter arose. My work, which I normally love, was developing its own heaviness. Most days and many evenings as well, I relate to some seventy congregations. Of all sorts and sizes, they gather in urban areas, press through suburbs, stretch out across rural landscapes. At times this company dances in its richness. I began now, though, to dwell on other matters these congregations face all the time. These include adjustment to life in a social environment that has changed radically over the past thirty years. They include the pain of stretching to find and share again the roots of a lively faith. They embrace seasons of struggle with difficult issues and times when communal life itself appears on the verge of fracture.

And so, both a coldness in the air and a mounting uneasiness over our common life prompted my examination of Christian community. Perhaps in this uncomplicated exercise I could spend more time with positive elements I sensed were out there. Perhaps this would yield some antidote to negative signals that seemed to cross my desk and my mind almost daily.

At the end of four months the experiment had grown into a graced addiction, and I could not stop. Seldom did I write for more than an hour. Always, though, experiences welled up and claimed attention. Many surprised me as they reappeared from the days just ended. I had hardly noticed them in passing. Now these often brief moments of community came vividly to life. A large number brought joy. Some chastened me. Others yielded times of deep gratitude.

By the end of the year, the experiences began to sort themselves. Certain patterns emerged, though none of these was yet fully formed. Underlying issues began to take shape, though none of these could I fully define. At this point the beckonings began.

On the most fundamental and persistent level, I felt

beckoned to recall that for Christians in general, and for me in particular, life shared in community with others is not optional. It is essential for the shaping of our lives and for our work in God's world. In the ancient biblical manuscripts when Jesus says, "You are the light of the world" (Matt. 5:14), he uses the plural "you." When he calls people to his side, he calls them into a personal relationship with himself; but he also calls them into relationship with one another.

Those of us who bear the name *Christian* are baptized into community. It is in community that we are formed. It is through community that we respond most effectively to the needs around us. Beneath my weekly pauses I could hear a summons to know once again how precious Christian community is and how utterly essential it is to living the way of Christ.

I began to hear also a more particular beckoning. There is, I believe, an almost desperate need for attentiveness to the presence of God in our common life. Much of today's devotional literature rightly focuses on rediscovering the extraordinary gifts of God in the ordinary moments of our lives. And again quite rightly much of the focus here is on the realm of personal experience. How shall we meet God once again in solitude and in our personal journeys? How does God break forth for us in such simple beauties as the crash of a wave or the fresh fragrance of a spring afternoon? In an age obsessed with haste, these issues are vital. At the same time, in an era parched by isolation and loneliness, are we not called to a renewed awareness of what God can do among people when they dare draw together?

A further beckoning arose from the weekly experiences themselves. I found that an event from one week would link with another from six weeks before and then with experiences from years ago. What were these graced episodes where God seemed, again and again, to stir up love? I could not make them happen, but could I at least name them? Could I grow more open to their presence and to the gift of community as God longs to give it? Both the joys and the intensity of the experiences now prompted a more detailed exploration of their particulars.

Finally, I received a beckoning to view the family of faith with fresh eyes. For most of my ministry I have looked at congregations and other faith communities primarily in terms of what they do. I have focused on their programs, activities, and outreach. While not entirely wrong, my preoccupation with the doing made me lose touch with a more fundamental level. I now found myself invited to look not so much on what we *do* as on how we *are* with one another; and how, in our simple ways of being, the Living Christ shapes us.

And so through the experiment came the beckonings; and as experiment and beckonings wove together, they gave rise to the pages that follow.

THE SHAPE OF THIS BOOK

Each of the chapters in this book offers a different angle from which to see the gift of community in Christ. Alone, no one of these angles is sufficient for a full viewing of the gift. Taken together, they at least hint at a more complete vision. They also probe issues which,

I believe, present themselves repeatedly to any person seeking to live more fully into the gift.

In preparing the chapters, I have not sought here to reproduce my journal notes from week to week. That would be tedious and, for purposes of this book, off the mark. I have hoped, rather, to evoke the themes and realities of Christian community as they appear to assert themselves again and again. My intent in writing has been not so much to define the territory as to affirm the splendid reality of God's gift of community and to encourage the readers' further prayerful exploration.

To aid in the exploration, following the essay portion of each chapter, readers will find

☞ *Reflection and Meditation*: For use personally or in a group setting, questions and reflective thoughts offered here will suggest avenues for further probing and for the sharing of insights.

☞ *Prayerful Exercises*: These prayerful practices and disciplines include some exercises for personal use and some for group use. They offer channels through which persons can grow in openness to the gifts and realities of Christian community.

Readers are, of course, free to choose among these as they feel led. In approaching Christian community, we encounter both mystery and gift. I am convinced that as we honestly explore community in whatever ways we find ourselves prayerfully drawn, both the mystery and the gift will only grow richer.

In all our explorations of Christian community, we are dealing ultimately with a grace, a treasure placed in our hands to be held by us collectively. We have not fashioned it. We cannot, of ourselves, make Christian community happen. And yet as we grow more able to see it, we may claim it more freely as it comes. In exploring its richness and detail, we move more deeply into its life. In these simple ways we ourselves may become channels for its nurture and its growth. My hope is that the following pages will, in some small way, open us for the seeing, the nurture, the growth of communal wholeness that the living God yearns to bring among us.

1

Beginnings...

I N A DEEP and fundamental sense, our immersion in
Christian community begins at the moment of baptism. The lives of others caringly surround us.
Water washes and marks us with the love of God. The
Holy Spirit claims us to the very depths of our being.
The community prays for us. And whether strong arms
cradle us and others speak words on our behalf or we
stand forth and confess the faith with our own lips, we
now enter an assembly whose immensity we only begin
to comprehend.

Time passes. Our journey of faith extends. We come
to know that God has surrounded our baptismal beginning with other beginnings as well. We may sense that
long before our baptism there arose within others, or
within us, a desire that we be joined to the community
of faith. This desire itself was a form of beginning.

At times our faith community may grow slack and
disappoint us. Or it may fill us with joy. Either way, in
hurt or in celebration, we find ourselves reaching for
greater fulfillment in the life we share with others. This
reaching too is a beginning. Or again, as we see some

21

act of communal faithfulness, Christian community
suddenly may clothe itself in garments of fresh meaning. We say, "There—that is what we are to be!" And
immediately upon speaking the words, we seek to follow more closely what we have just witnessed. This
also is a beginning.

I believe that our beginnings in Christian community are recurrent. Baptism takes place at a particular
moment. Yet that moment remains with us. We draw
life and meaning from it again and again. Our other
beginnings in community are frequently the same in
this regard. Whether their exact contours press into our
lives many times or just once, they become vehicles for
our ongoing illumination. They are root for us. They are
foundation. They are special realms where the living
God shapes and molds us for the life we share.

In a later chapter, we will look directly on the sacra-
mental gift of baptism as a channel for the formation of
our life in community. At this point, I would like to
explore three other beginnings God offers and stirs
among us. I find these etched with particular sharp-
ness in our current cultural situation. They are a *hunger*
of spirit that awakens us to our longing for community
in Christ; the *holy gift* of Christian community that can
both startle and feed us in the midst of our hunger; a
quality of *awareness* that, when accepted and cultivated,
can allow us to see more clearly the holy gift of
Christian community and to live into it more freely.

HUNGER

Several years ago a pastor and good friend of mine
found himself, much to his surprise, under considera-

tion for a call to a new congregation. His present situation fulfilled and challenged him, but the committee members from the other church pressed him and his wife to pay their church a visit. The couple received great encouragement from the committee during their stay and began to sense that they should be open to an invitation to move if it came. "We'll be in touch with you soon," the committee chair said, smiling broadly.

On returning home the couple entered an earnest time of prayerful discernment. Much about the new situation attracted them. Much continued to excite them where they were. They also embarked upon an unexpected period of waiting. Two weeks passed. Then two more. Finally at the end of six weeks, the minister arrived home one afternoon to find a curt message on his answering device: "Hello, Reverend? I'm calling from the committee. We...uh...enjoyed meeting you, but we feel we're being led someplace else." That was it. No "thank you"—not even a well wishing or an apology for the delay.

The couple handled the situation well. However, my friend did raise a poignant question as he reflected on the long wait and the brief message left on his answering machine. "Have we in the church forgotten to be gracious to one another?"

This question, innocently asked, hovers around a great deal of brokenness in the church. For many of us, the hunger for community in Christ is a hunger for its restoration. Do we often enough speak and hear the words of grace? Do we care for one another on the levels that we really can? Have we, perhaps not meaning to at all, forgotten to be gracious? Underneath such questions lies an ache for sensitivities that seem to have vanished.

The hunger for community in Christ mounts if we experience division in our own particular faith community. It may deepen as we witness the widespread nature of such divisions. The fracturing of a congregation, once rare, is now common. Those of us in denominational roles gird our loins with all the conflict resolution skills we can muster. While we need the skills and churches need help with the conflicts bound to arise in any body of persons, the growth of conflict within congregations is a disturbing sign. The thought *It will only get worse* may course through our minds even if we do not speak the words aloud.

Beyond the matter of conflict within congregations, many of us live with divisions that slice through the very center of our denominations. At times these divisions are handled with care and deep prayer. At times they grow sharp, leaving a bitter taste. And again in pew and pulpit, we ache for a vanished wholeness.

The manifestation of such aching is ever personal and particular. One day I was present at a Bible study. The leader asked what needs the group members felt most intimately. A young mother answered instantly and with much feeling: "My need is for community in Christ. I crave it." The silence that followed was the silence of assent and recognition.

A few days later I listened as a friend struggled with whether to stay in his denominational position. "What we desperately need to attend on in the church is our relationships, and yet my work only gets more and more bureaucratic. We have aimed ourselves in the wrong direction and don't seem to be able to stop." We feel such things in the stomach and the heart. They grab us and will not let go.

The hunger we feel within the church is, of course, cousin to a hunger rampant in the society that surrounds us. Fractures within churches and denominations mirror fractures in the broader culture. Distrust of congregational and denominational leaders finds its echo in the distrust voiced loudly in a variety of political and economic arenas. And beneath the brokenness and distrust lies once again the persistent yearning for a nearly evaporated closeness.

Theologian Douglas John Hall cites what he calls "the quest for meaningful community" as being among the major pursuits of the society that surrounds us. The quest is particularly acute due to a dual failure: the failure of individualism and the failure of most forms of community. Individualism has played a vital role in asserting rights and claiming freedoms, but it cannot adequately address the major economic and ecological issues that press upon our world. These cry out for the shared response of community. As for community, though, it flounders: "We have witnessed the failure of most forms of communality—dramatically so in Eastern Europe, but also in our own society, where deep cynicism informs all public life and institutions."[1] And so the society around us too hungers for a closeness it has lost and seemingly does not know how to find again.

⸎

"We're like this," a woman said. With both hands she formed a series of imaginary clumps on the table that lay between the two of us. Each clump was separate and distant from the others. "We're like this in the church now. And we're like this in our society. We live in little bunches that don't much connect." She worked for a community agency. She was a devout member of her Christian congregation. She knew both worlds. We stared at the imaginary clumps. We were quiet. For the moment, the clumps came together only in her yearning.

HOLY GIFT

It is as we feel the ache of hunger for community that a further beginning meets us. Unlike the hunger for community, which we know most intensely within, this beginning wells up from beyond us. Appearing on the horizon of our lives, it moves directly toward the inner hunger. It touches us deeply and offers hints as to the satisfaction of our hunger. This further beginning is the moment, any moment, when we receive the goodness of community in Christ.

The moments of Christian community often come as a surprise. They break in when we are not expecting much of anything. They catch our minds. They hook our attention. Unless we choose to set them aside, they will not leave us alone after they have passed.

Often the moments of community in Christ are disarmingly simple. At an Ash Wednesday service, congregants had just written words of personal confession on small sheets of paper and placed them in a large bowl in the front of the sanctuary. The pastor had ignited them with a match. A toddler, overwhelmed by curiosity, dashed up to look at the flaming bowl. He arrived just as a ninety-year-old man earnestly dropped his paper into the flames. The toddler crashed into the back of the man's legs. The child's mother gasped. For a moment, both figures swayed. Then, with great gentleness, the man took the child's hand and they stood together, looking at the now subsiding fire. Those who witnessed this event saw far more than just a pleasant scene. By some miracle the two stood captivated, hand in hand, present to the all-consuming mercies of God. The image hovered in our minds long after the two parted.

Often the places of community in Christ are utterly modest. We fall ill. Another person visits us and prays. We struggle with grief, and others call or write the simplest of notes. All is so quickly and inconspicuously done. And yet in such times we are deeply blessed.

The gift of community comes even in untidy meetings. We struggle with a painful situation. Does a church member need correcting? our pastor? or the members' fading zeal for mission that, my heavens, needs to be pumped up yet again? We contend with the issue at hand. We tussle with one another in the process. And then despite our slogging pace, it happens. It may catch us as we close with prayer. It may break forth as we stare at our hands during an awkward silence. We suddenly sense a closeness. Unexpectedly, we see the goodness of the others who have gathered. We feel grateful—grateful to be included, grateful for the bonds. And even if we don't dare say it aloud, we are grateful for the Living Christ who has been in the midst of our sharing. The moment may pass, but it does not fully leave us.

Such places of community in Christ do not depend upon a particular set of feelings. During my initial year of asking "Where have I seen it?" the places of Christian community were scarce some weeks and bountiful others. Thin or thick, the mix varied greatly and pointed to something beyond all feeling as the identifying mark. A candlelight demonstration for the homeless...a congregation grieving for the sudden death of a beloved leader...women of all races, arms linked, shouting the joy of their oneness...a quiet, loving vigil for those living with AIDS—beneath the vast array of feelings embraced by such diverse gatherings flowed a single message: "Right here, we are in Christ. As we weep, as we laugh, as we act, he is among us."

The source of all such coming together is surely Jesus himself. Community is ever his gift. It was this way from the start. He formed the table fellowship. He sent his followers out not alone but in the company of one another. When he came upon them after the Resurrection, he joined two on the road, encouraged a frightened crew huddled behind locked doors, fed a hungry band of them at dawn on the shores of Galilee. He initially had drawn persons together, and he continued to shape them as a body. When the Holy Spirit burned forth Pentecost, it settled not on one but on a whole assembly.

In lyrical words the letter to the Ephesians traces the full sweep of this gift:

> So then you are no longer strangers and aliens, but you are citizens with the saints and also members of the household of God, built upon the foundation of the apostles and prophets, with Christ Jesus himself as the cornerstone. In him the whole structure is joined together and grows into a holy temple in the Lord; in whom you also are built together spiritually into a dwelling place for God (2:19-22).

In Christ Jesus we are formed into one people stretching through the ages of time. And in this sense, the
community he creates is not only a gift. It is holy. That
is, its source is not in us. It emanates from him.
Community sweeps forth and claims us from the
realms of grace.

If we view the source of community from a slightly
different angle and take in the full sweep of the biblical
history, we see that God relentlessly applies the
covenant. God forms a covenant with Abraham and
Sarah in order that their offspring will grow great in
number and become a blessing to all the earth. At
Mount Sinai, God draws together the children of Israel
and again makes a covenant that this particular people
might offer blessing. And when persons repeatedly
shatter the covenant and the fellowship comes undone,
God does not stop. In Jesus, God offers a new covenant
and draws together a people so that they might be
ambassadors of reconciliation in a fractured world. Our
coming together is not of us; it is of God. Its steady
birth is not of our manufacture; God's longing love
gives birth to community.

In this context, even our smallest moments of coming together in Christ are a holy gift. They are the fruit
of his work among us. They are a sign of what he seeks
to draw forth.

⌁

The two of them sat together for at least an hour. He did
most of the talking. She, a friend, listened. With much
pain, he poured out the events of the past three months.
His father had died unexpectedly. Soon afterward his

mother's Alzheimer's disease appeared to grow much worse. "Or perhaps with Dad gone, it's just easier for all of us to see." Independent of these matters, stress had mounted substantially at his place of employment, and now one of his children faced a serious medical problem.

For a time the man talked of these situations as he much needed to. Then he started to speak of others who, to his surprise, were reaching out to him. Their small, caring gestures affected him profoundly. Friends in the church brought food. An older brother to whom he felt particularly close offered to pray with him. People from a church he once joined in another state now called and shared their support.

At length his friend had to go. He asked if they might pray together. She said, "Yes." For a long time they sat in quietness. When he spoke, he shared a single sentence. "I thank you, God, for your great gift of connecting our lives."

AWARENESS

Our movement into Christian community begins both in hunger and in holy gift. Hunger for community prompts our search. The holy gift of community in Christ meets us in our hunger; it nourishes us even as it invites our continued searching. And if we fully respond to the hunger, if we thoroughly explore the gift, we find ourselves drawn to a third place of beginning: awareness.

In his short story "Homecoming," author Barry Lopez writes of botanist Wick Colter.[2] As a graduate student, Colter achieves international status for redefining an entire family of plants. Honored for his brilliance, he begins to travel and lecture widely, writing nonstop. He keeps up this pace for several years. Then one day, as he walks with his daughter through the woods, he discovers that he has forgotten the names even of the simplest flowers. His daughter becomes his teacher. That night Colter returns to the woods. He lies on the damp earth and inhales the cool air. He feels prickers against his wrist and gently fingers soft, growing forms. He is rediscovering. He is recovering a fundamental awareness.

Much of what the Christian community needs right now is to recover fundamental awareness. At a denominational gathering not long ago a national church leader lamented, "Everything is critiqued today. That is all we seem to do." The comment was, I believe, much on target and pertinent to far more than his particular denomination. Critique lets us dissect. It lets us stand at a distance. It lets us pull matters apart. Fundamentally, critique lets us ask, "What is wrong?" and possibly, "How can we make it better?"

Awareness follows a more subtle and comprehensive path. Where critique presses, awareness waits. Where critique judges and tries to control, awareness opens to receive all that is emerging. Critique separates itself from events. Awareness immerses in them, vulnerable to whatever is taking place. In its most complete expression in both Eastern and Western spiritual traditions, awareness is the quality of simple alertness and receptivity to whatever the Divine Presence may be doing.

Jesus seeks to draw people into a fuller state of awareness with the words we know nearly by heart:

> "Let the little children come to me, and do not stop them;
> for it is to such as these that the kingdom of God belongs.

Truly I tell you, whoever does not receive the kingdom of God as a little child will never enter it" (Luke 18:16-17).

We are to become like the awed and the open, like those blinking their eyes at the wonder of life. Do this, Jesus counsels, and then we shall enter most fully what God sets before us. Not long before his crucifixion, Jesus responds to those seeking dramatic signs of God's reign:

"The kingdom of God is not coming with things that can be observed; nor will they say, 'Look, here it is!' or 'There it is!' For, in fact, the kingdom of God is among you" (Luke 17:20-21).

Be open, Jesus counsels. Be attentive. Be aware! The reign of God is in our very midst.

Theologian Dietrich Bonhoeffer offered a similar counsel of awareness. For a small community of seminary students seeking to live faithfully amid the horrors of Nazism, he wrote:

If we do not give thanks daily for the Christian fellowship in which we have been placed, even where there is no great experience,...if on the contrary, we only keep complaining to God that everything is so paltry and petty, so far from what we expected, then we hinder God from letting our fellowship grow according to the measure and riches which are there for us all in Jesus Christ....

The more thankfully we daily receive what is given to us, the more surely and steadily will fellowship increase and grow from day to day as God pleases.[3]

Be open to the goodness. Receive it. Cherish it, for in that tiny goodness and through the interweaving of our thankful hearts, the holy gift of community shall grow.

Awareness, even under severe circumstances, lets

us know more fully the holy gift of Christian community. It allows us to sense community's many nuances and forms. It opens us once again to the Spirit that draws us into community, even as we name more honestly our hunger. And through all of this, awareness frees us to live joyfully into the gift wherever it may suddenly flourish.

Becoming aware humbles us, putting us flat on the ground with faces close to the earth. It thrusts us back to where we started. Like children, we must learn again what surrounds us. With our lives we touch afresh the grace-filled forms we had almost forgotten. In turn, they draw us forth. It is all a modest, unassuming enterprise. It is also, I sense, the beginning of a deeper formation in the life we share together.

REFLECTION AND MEDITATION

1. What general hungers for community do you see in the society around you?

2. What hunger for community in Christ have you known in your own spiritual journey?

3. Think on one occasion when you have experienced the gift of Christian community. What was this like? What happened?

4. What do you believe keeps us from seeing the gift of community in Christ when it lies close at hand?

5. Think of times when you became aware just by being still of beauty around you, of the goodness of another person, of the bonds between your life and

the lives of others. What were these times of awareness like? What allowed them to happen?

PRAYERFUL EXERCISES

A Prayerful Exploration of Hunger for Community
(*personal or group*)

If a group shares in this exercise, a leader may invite persons through the various steps, allowing extended times for quiet and prayerful reflection.

1. After a time of coming to quiet, ask God to let you see persons around you who hunger for the bonds of community. Let their hungers come into your mind. Take time with the hungers. Be present to what you see.

2. In quietness ask God to let you see your own hungers for community. Let any come forth in your personal life and journey, in your life with your family of faith, in your life with the wider community.

3. Draw forth now what has been given you. If you are alone, you may wish to write down any particular hungers that you have seen and that have caught hold of your concern. If you are in a group, share with others as you feel led and are comfortable.

4. Close with a time of thanksgiving for any fresh understanding you have received and with prayers for an openness to God's presence in the midst of the hunger for community.

An Exploration of Community in Christ (*personal*)

1. In quietness and prayerfulness, reflect, "Where have I most truly felt myself in Christian community with another/others?" Let two or three special times of such community come to mind. Name them. Take time to be present to them, to recall again what happened, to look on them in gratitude.

2. Prayerfully reflect, "What blessings have come to me personally through these occasions of community in Christ?" Note any reflections that come to mind.

3. Now ask, "What blessings appear to have come to others through these special places or moments of community in Christ?" Once more, note any reflections that come to mind.

4. Close with a time of quiet gratitude for any moments of community you have recalled, for any blessings that have come through them, and for any insights you have received.

An Exploration of Community in Christ (*group*)

1. After a time of quietness, read together John 13:34-35:

    "I give you a new commandment, that you love one another. Just as I have loved you, you also should love one another. By this everyone will know that you are my disciples, if you have love for one another."

2. Go about the group allowing each person to share one occasion or more when she or he has experienced Christian community.

3. Reflect together: What are the varieties of communal experience among us? What does this variety have to say to us as individuals? as a community of faith?

4. Now prayerfully reflect, "What seems to have encouraged or allowed these experiences of Christian community?" After a period of quietness, share your responses.

5. Close with a time of quiet thankfulness for the experiences shared and for any fresh insights received through one another. Read again John 13:34-35.

A Discipline of Reflection and Awareness
(*personal or group*)

☞ Covenant for a fixed period of time, two months or more, when you will pause once a week to write down any instances of Christian community in the preceding days.

☞ Be open in this process, and relaxed. Enter the time of writing prayerfully. Some weeks much may emerge, some weeks little. On occasion you may be given to see more of what harms community than what builds it. This too will be a gift of awareness.

☞ If you follow this exercise alone, after several weeks take time to reflect on any patterns of understanding that appear to emerge.

☞ If you make a commitment with others to follow this exercise, come together at least once a month to share what you are seeing and learning.

☞ Take time at the close of each exploration to offer thanks for what you have seen and to ask that you may continue to grow in awareness of the gift of community.

2
Simple
Places...

MANY YEARS ago when I was in my teens and passing some weeks at a summer camp, I spent one afternoon on what was billed as a "photographic horseback ride." A young counselor gathered about twenty of us after rest hour, watched as we saddled our horses, and then gave quick, firm instructions: "Keep your cameras ready. When you see something beautiful, take pictures!" That was it, nothing more. This brief orientation over and done with, he led us out along the trail.

During the next hour we passed slowly over a sagebrush strewn flatland and several low ridges, through a dry gully, along banks of a braided stream, and up and then down the side of a large butte. Soft greens, dusty browns, sparkling silvers shone from the landscape around us. Brilliant puffs of cumulus clouds moved gently against an azure sky.

At length the counselor drew us into a circle. "What did you get?" he asked. No response. "Any pictures?" No response. "Not one?" Still no response. "You mean you actually didn't see anything to photograph?" At this point we campers began to engage in a variety of activities, such as clearing our throats, lowering our heads, and fiddling purposefully with our cameras. The counselor grumbled, "I can't believe you missed all that good stuff!" With this he gave his horse a solid nudge and started the whole bunch of us back toward camp.

The ride took about twenty minutes. We went at a quick pace. All along the way the sound of horses' hooves was punctuated by the clicking of small cameras.

⟿⟾

Christian community, like beauty, often presents itself in the intimate, the common, the close at hand. It comes to bud and flower in the simplest of places. Race by, and we miss it. Wait to see it in some idealized state, and we pass without knowing it is there.

On the matter of beauty, our counselor was nothing if not direct: "I can't believe you missed all that good stuff!" On the matter of Christian community, Jesus was just as direct and even more pointed: "Where two or three are gathered in my name, I am there among them" (Matt. 18:20). These words clearly contain a counsel of simplicity. As Jesus' followers, if we are to find true community with one another and with him, then we should look not just to the massive throng or the dramatic moment. We should look as well to the simplest instance of one life brushing up against another. We should open ourselves to the small and intimate moments when persons draw together in their joys and in their needs.

In addition to containing a counsel of simplicity, Jesus' words offer a clear statement regarding the intent of our coming together: "For where two or three are gathered *in my name*, I am there among them" (*italics added*). It is not just a matter of gathering together. We do a great deal of that in our society. We gather to watch a game. We gather to shake our heads in distress over what somebody else in the office has done. We assemble to sing or to dance, to eat or to play. The best of such comings together may be healthful, invigorating, uplifting. Other times of joining together may be petty or just plain dull. For even the most enlivening of events, though, Jesus' words point to a deeper dimension. For true Christian community, we are to gather "in his name."

In this chapter I would like to explore the simple places of our gathering in his name. What are they? Where are they found during the passage of a day or a year or a season of life? What blessings come as we, in Christ, enter them? What really does it mean that in the simplest of ways we gather in his name? I ask these questions not to busy our minds. I ask them in the belief that exploring some of the answers can further open us to the immediacy of Christian community.

Biblical scholar Paul S. Minear once observed, "The NT idea of the church is not so much a technical doctrine as a gallery of pictures."[1] What follows here is just that: pictures, quick panoramas, gleanings from five realms spotted along the pathway of my own somewhat limited explorations. These offerings are suggestive rather than exhaustive or definitive. Other persons scanning the landscape will, doubtless, have fresh scenes to share. What I have perceived of Christ's presence in the simplest of communal forms brings me great joy. Part of this joy lies in knowing that others will, as they look on what follows, be able to speak of things I have missed entirely.

TASK

As I look back over notes from a year of consciously opening to the places of Christian community, I am struck by how often task is the place of community's birth. The variety of such birthplaces appears to be limitless. Three persons gather prayerfully to address an issue of deep pain in their wider congregation. The task for them is healing. A group of pastors, men and women with many years of service among them, spend two days in worship and discussion as they explore how to serve faithfully in the time of their "retirement." Their task is discernment. Members of a church group, ranging in age from seven to seventy-two, laugh as they pile hammers, boards, nails, and a chest full of sandwiches into the back of two pickup trucks. They continue to laugh as they head off to repair a neighborhood shelter. Their task is to build.

The blessings that come to the faith community gathered about a task are often modest in their definition and deep in their realization. These blessings include the following: a fuller knowing of one another, a merging of gifts, a blending of personality, a yielding of fruits.

The time we spend with others on a common task is surely a time of growing to know and to be known in the innermost places of our lives. As we labor we talk. We listen. We share and are silent together. As we rest from the task, and even while the task is going forth, conversation opens windows on our personal joys, our hopes, our families, our needs. When we find the task daunting, we learn the grace of acknowledging this to one another. And if the task goes with unexpected smoothness, we celebrate. In all of this, we come to know one another on a deeper, freer level than we have before.

Personal gifts merge in the performance of task. The gifts I do not have, another does. What I lack, another will supply. And what I do have to give can, in some small way, find its own place in the larger offering. As we share in a task, however simple it may be, we repeatedly see the truth of Paul's teaching that we are the body of Christ and each an indispensable part of the whole (1 Cor. 12). One person's sense of humor by itself is a fine gift. So is the ability of another to make plans. So is the ability of yet another to cook. Each gift is good in and of itself. When gifts are drawn together in a common task, the richness of each gift increases greatly. Planning becomes a source of ongoing guidance for all; the mastery of cooking provides others and the cook with much needed nourishment; the humor becomes leaven and lightness for the entire group.

As a task proceeds, personalities blend. To say this is to say something quite different from saying personalities merge. To merge is to lose identity. It is to rub out all distinctiveness. It is to erase all the rough edges, obliterate all the interesting contours and intriguing boundaries. To blend personalities is to keep distinctiveness and create a new, often spicier, mix. Minimally, it means that in the task at hand we learn to work together—warts, eccentricities, and all. Beyond this, it may mean that such disparate qualities as grumpiness and naivete, intensity and childlike wonder wind up in an utterly unexpected dance of mutual appreciation and creativity.

And we experience the fruits. If the task goes well, these include the obvious fruit of achievement: a project completed, a problem solved, an issue addressed. If the task does not go as desired, then we may gather the fruit of communal learning from the experience. And either way, we receive the fruits of deepened bonds, merged gifts, and lives more blended, less separate than before.

What is the "in Christness" of all of this interaction? What determines whether a communal task is "in my name" and not merely a job undertaken by a group? The answer, as I have watched for it, appears to be twofold. First, no matter how small the task, the group involved acknowledges its own desire to be in Christ. This happens simply: a prayer; a saying of grace; time spent, individually and collectively, reflecting on the desire to open to Christ both in deed and in spirit. Focusing not just on the task itself but also on the root of all such tasks, the group members allow themselves to be shaped by the One in whose name they work.

Second, when the task is completed, the group releases it thankfully. The community that undertook the task yields it as a gift back to the One in whose spirit the community has sought to act. The community then moves on, grateful for the gifts of spirit it has received during its common undertaking.

ILLNESS

For members of the Christian community, illness is as much a presence as it is for any other persons. If we take care of our bodies, then perhaps we shall avoid unnecessary advances of illness. If we exercise, watch our diet, and get our rest, we may sidestep the havoc wrought by our society's penchant for overindulgence. If we are good stewards of our health, then we may enjoy the gifts of stamina and strength. We know full well, though, that despite our best efforts, illness can break in unexpectedly. It may come as a distinct annoyance; and due to a bad cold or a fever, we are unable to attend a long anticipated event. Far more serious, illness may suddenly slice to the center of our being or threaten another whose life is as dear as our own. When this occurs, all plans pass into shadow; and we are wrung to the core.

What increasingly strikes me about the Christian community and illness is not the presence or absence of illness itself. Illness, like joy and loss, woe and celebration, is bound to be with us. What catches and moves me is seeing how illness can become an opportunity for our collective deepening in Christ. To say this is not to paint illness in bright colors, but it is to note that even the time of severe sickness can become a graced season for drawing yet closer together in the One who eternally surrounds us.

Often the drawing together is spontaneous. It arises as a movement of the heart that we must obey. So we send a card, write a letter, place a phone call. The "in-Christness" of these actions is wholly natural. We act prayerfully, knowing that the card, the letter, the call cannot accomplish all that we desire. Yet after we take our admittedly inadequate step, we know that in some way our life and the life of the other have, by Christ, been linked on a level far deeper than anything accomplished by our outward act alone.

A colleague came into my office one morning to let me know she had just received a phone call reporting a friend's diagnosis of terminal cancer. "I thought you'd want to know," she said. A little later I walked by my colleague's office and noticed it was empty. Two hours later she was standing in my door again. "I was going to call and say, 'I'm so sorry about your diagnosis,' but then I knew that I needed to go and put my arms around my friend. I needed that for both of us." The tone of her voice declared the essence of what had taken place: Even in the midst of awkwardness and sorrow, their coming together had been healing and rich.

Often the ill themselves give the greatest gifts to the community of faith. They humbly offer their quiet, unobtrusive gifts. We visit them wishing to bring encouragement and then find ourselves encouraged. We cannot figure out what words to say, but they do. We struggle with our faith but then discover their faith to be a source of guidance for our own. One by one, life by life, they enrich us. And the enrichment we receive is the enrichment of attending on one whose life with Christ informs our own.

Ultimately, illness becomes a domain where we can learn collectively to lean on the Living Christ. We may do this in simplicity, the well and the ill alike. We may do it in spoken prayer. We may do it sitting together in total silence, hands held and hearts yearning. In the process we begin to comprehend that the bounty of our community in Christ has little to do with particular outcomes and favorable diagnoses. It does not depend on bad news or good. The caring union of even two or three lives in Christ comes to be seen for what it truly is: a bond sustained eternally, infinitely nourished, and infinitely nourishing us through even the most parched and aching seasons of our lives.

CONVERSATION

One Sunday afternoon as I reflected on the question, "Where have I seen Christian community this past week?" the answer came in a series of four images. In all four images I found myself in conversation with another: a woman pastor with whom I had dined the Wednesday night before; an older gentleman I had chanced to talk with the next day following a long meeting; a friend who bear-hugged me after I had shared a hurt; a gifted young man who, to my surprise, invited me into the place of his own searching.

The images grew both distinctive and intertwined as I watched. The distinctiveness appeared as we followed the varied courses of our conversations. In one we explored a personal pain. In another, and in words that surprised both of us, we shared new and exciting experiences of grace. With the older gentleman I mostly listened as he, with much animation, described fresh possibilities for ministry among the young and the poor. In the fourth instance the other person and I traced the emerging shape of a call to new forms of service.

The intertwining came on the level of each conversation's outcome. In some way each had carried both me and, it appeared, the other to a new understanding in our Christian faith. Not that the change in our faith had been dramatic or revolutionary. It was not in any of the four instances. Yet as I looked back, I realized that in each conversation faith's journey had been the underlying theme of our words; in each instance we had drawn close in our sharing; in each the words and insights of the other had stretched the boundaries of our own journeys.

Experiences such as these have awakened me to certain passages of scripture that I must admit I had long ago set aside as sounding, well, overly tight. From Ephesians we read,

> Let no evil talk come out of your mouths, but only what is useful for building up, as there is need, so that your words may give grace to those who hear (4:29).

And again:

> Entirely out of place is obscene, silly, and vulgar talk; but instead, let there be thanksgiving (5:4).

And more gently from the letter to the Colossians:

> Let the word of Christ dwell in you richly; teach and admonish one another in all wisdom; and with gratitude in your hearts sing psalms, hymns, and spiritual songs to God (3:16).

For years passages such as these conjured in my mind scenes of pale and lifeless gatherings. Maybe a little singing, but please, no laughter or levity. Don't speak unless you have something profound to say; and if it is profound, let it be heavy as well.

I suppose such spiritual dryness can be wrung from these words. What I hear from them now, though, is not a constricting of our conversations but rather an opening to what our conversations can embrace. Conversation may become the place of unexpected edification, spontaneous thanksgiving, suddenly imparted grace.

The above counsels of hallowed conversation build on an ancient tradition of the faith community:

> Hear, O Israel: The Lord is our God, the Lord alone. You shall love the Lord your God with all your heart, and with all your soul, and with all your might. Keep these words that I am commanding you today in your heart. Recite them to your children and talk about them when you are at home and when you are away, when you lie down and when you rise. (Deut. 6:4-7)

Even the great teaching that the Lord alone is God was known in the closeness of the heart and the directness of conversation as one moved through the day. One was to talk of it while sitting in the house, walking by the way, lying down and rising.

The gathering of our lives to Christ as we converse can be utterly natural. It may happen spontaneously as we eat dessert, share a glass of wine, or watch a sunset. It may come to pass in planned settings as spiritual friends meet for an intended conversation or as colleagues sit about a lighted candle, hear scripture, and share their stories. Whatever the circumstance, and whatever the promptings of grace, we speak of our faith or of our journey in Christ or of questions that burn within us. We may talk for only a brief time, but Christ is in our words and in our hearts. We leave the conversation blessed, and what we have received lives long within us.

We cannot doggedly force such moments; we cannot make them happen. What occurs of grace and community in conversation happens when we speak freely out of our heartfelt yearnings and joys. My own concern, though, has little to do with forcing the matter. Reticence to speak at all is, I believe, far more the danger. Shyness of expression is more steadily the norm for me and, I suspect, for many others.

The faces of four persons came into my mind one Sunday afternoon as I reflected on where community in Christ had shown itself in the preceding days. Each person had dared to lean on the Spirit and speak. By grace, I too had leaned and spoken. "Where two or three are gathered...." Four persons. Four graced moments. I wondered at the immediacy of it all. And I wondered as well, "Do I dare, do we dare, let this happen as much as it can?"

INNER CHURCH

Many years ago I heard a great and, on the matter of civil rights, courageous minister speak of what he called the "inner church." In effect his words were these:

> You all have an "inner church." The inner church is that special gathering of folks who nourished you in your own faith. They taught you. They set examples. They showed courage. And now you carry them around inside of you. They still teach you and set examples. They still encourage you. Some of you even talk with them! That's not a bad idea. Your inner church. Take a look. Who is in your inner church?

The question before twenty lay leaders one Saturday morning differed only slightly. They had gathered for a day of prayer and reflection. After opening worship, each lay leader was asked to write the name of one person who had grown spiritually and who, in the process of that growth, had enriched the lay leader's personal faith also. All were then invited to continue in silence and consider: How did that person grow? What gifts of spirit has she or he given to you?

I watched. That really was my only role. As quietness deepened, I could see expressions playing across a few faces. A smile. A wistfulness. A brightening of the eyes here and there. Some jotted notes.

At length each group member was invited to share as she or he wished. Persons could remain silent, pass, or speak aloud of the one who had grown and had in some way affected their own lives. As matters worked out, the sharing took nearly two hours. Some laughed as they talked. Two wept. All spoke. No one wearied of listening.

At the end of the sharing, the group was surrounded by a company better than twice its size. The new arrivals included a woman who had taught first grade in 1920; several grandparents, aunts, and uncles; a child who had died three years before; a deacon who, likewise, had died two decades before; a corporation president who put workers' needs ahead of personal profit. On and on the line of them came. As the group broke for lunch, the participants appeared much enlivened by the company that had joined them from within.

There is, of course, no way fully to delineate the firm reality we deal with here. All our attempts at description ultimately point to its mystery. The Celts cherished what we now might call spiritual friends, persons who even beyond the grave could be lively, active sources of aid. One could pray to them, seek their guidance, receive their support.[2] The writer of the Letter to the

Hebrews lists a near avalanche of leaders in the faith and then concludes,

> Therefore, since we are surrounded by so great a cloud of witnesses, let us also lay aside every weight and the sin that clings so closely, and let us run with perseverance the race that is before us (12:1).

I heard an older man read that text once. He had a brilliant mind and a long history of devoted service to migrant workers and the urban poor. "The cloud of witnesses!" he said to the group of us who had gathered. "The cloud of witnesses! They're all right here!" One look at his face caused us to sense, "Yes. No question about it!"

For me, though, the phrase *inner church* has been particularly helpful. Like all metaphors, it lets me sort my thoughts on a matter that human speech will never fully contain. And for however long I must deal with human speech, the members of my inner church will continue to come and offer themselves as my guides and encouragers: grandmother...parents...friend who died at sixteen...aunts and uncles...a teacher who whistled and laughed because of the faith that was in him. I can't say who will be there tomorrow. I only know that the gift of "two or three gathering" is at times closer even than memory and incontestably alive.

TIME

At this point I am reminded of the "It doesn't fit" test a lot of us took when we were going into first grade. I think the test had something to do with measuring our intelligence, but in all the years since I have never quite been able to figure that out. Anyway, some kindly adult we had not seen before came into our kindergarten and passed out booklets filled with small pictures. Over breakfast parents had already told us, "Drink all of your orange juice today" and "Don't worry about what happens at school this morning; it's not all that important"—both signs that the grown-up world was up to something major.

Once she made sure we all knew how to hold a pencil, the stranger spoke very slowly and said, "In this book you will see four pictures in a row. On each row, three of the things fit, and one does not. Please circle the one that does not fit." We looked at the pictures. Sure enough, on the first row we saw a dog, a kitten, a rabbit, and a slingshot. On the second row we spotted a locomotive, a motorcycle, a racing car, and somebody who looked vaguely like our mother. After sucking our erasers, we circled the slingshot and Mother. From there on things got rougher, but given the sense that somehow our lives were swaying in the wind, we all felt we were off to a pretty good start.

In considering simple places where we can know the grace of Christian community, we have four items to which here is added a fifth: *task, illness, conversation, inner church*, and now *time*. The first four fit. As we regard each of them with our mind's eye, we can see people— sometimes two, sometimes three, sometimes more. Actions take place. The fulfillment of Christ's presence is at least possible in the interpersonal exchanges. But what of time? Time sounds abstract. Time suggests no images of persons working and relating, comforting and speaking. How does time fit here, if at all?

I must admit that time never entered my mind as an

ingredient in Christ's community until I noted that it kept arising in conversations I had with others. This happened in little, unexpected ways. One day I asked several friends where they had seen the blessings of Christian community. The oldest answered with a deeply personal story involving three persons and their gradual growth through a series of experiences. "Without time," he concluded, "long time, I'm not sure any of this would have occurred."

I found myself sharing a meal with a small group of congregational leaders who had, to put it gently, been at one another's throats and mine only eighteen months before. Now we listened to one another, prayed, laughed. "We needed to take time together," offered one who had been among the angriest. That was all she said. Time. I thought on what time had meant in this situation. It meant time just to eat with one another. And time to talk. Time to struggle and stay with one another through the months of distress. Time to call on the phone when we learned that one of our group was in need or in pain.

It is not so much a matter of how time "fits" with the other elements in this chapter. It is rather a matter of what time provides for them. Time affords us the opportunity to immerse, to grow, to deepen in the simple bonds we share. Like so much else, time is a gift to us. As such, it may become a graced realm for knowing Christ and one another. And for all the realms of our simple gathering—task and illness, conversation and inner church—time is the environment in which our oneness in Christ can gently and steadily grow.

Time will return as a factor in later chapters, particularly as we explore "Practices," "Conflict," and "Hallowed Days and Seasons." For now, though, I feel compelled to introduce the matter of time on its own. Time is intimately bound with even the simplest occurrences of Christian communal life. And the question is not, "How does time fit with the elemental places of our gathering in Christ?" It is rather, "How, through time, are we being deepened, taught, stretched in even the simplest of these places?"

REFLECTION AND MEDITATION

1. Where have you encountered community in Christ through a task? an illness? a conversation? inner church? What blessings came through these encounters?

2. Where have any of these simple experiences of Christian community grown deeper through time?

3. What other simple realms of experience would you add to the list shared in this chapter? How have you come to know them? What have they offered you? And what have you offered through them?

4. Which special disciplines or habits have helped you become aware of the simple moments of Christian community? Can you think of anything that might help you become more aware of these moments than you are now?

PRAYERFUL EXERCISES

Awareness of the Simple Places of Community in Christ
(*personal*)

Persons may wish to follow this form of personal exploration once or twice, noting what comes forth. The greatest growth in awareness, though, will come where the practice is adopted as a simple discipline of prayerful exploration for a period of four or more weeks.

1. After a time of quieting, ask that you may be aware of any occasions in the past twenty-four hours when you and possibly just one or two others have "gathered in my name." Let anything come to mind where you and another, or others, have been in Christ—perhaps in a conversation, a task, or in contact during an illness—or in some other simple act of drawing together.

2. If nothing has come to mind, merely ask that you may remain open to any small gifts of community that God may give.

3. If any gift of community comes to mind, take time to be present to it. Recall its goodness. How did it come to you? How have you grown aware of its specialness.

4. Whether or not the past twenty-four hours appear to have contained simple places of being with others in Christ, close with thanksgiving for the desire to see such places and prayer to grow in awareness of any such places as they arise in the passage of a day.

Meditation on the Growth of Christian Community through Time (*personal or group*)

1. Personally, or in a group, select some time period in the life of your community of faith. You may want to choose a set number of months or even years. You may wish to focus on a time frame defined by some special set of circumstances, such as a season of major change, conflict, or healing.

2. In quietness, prayerfully reflect on this time. Let come forth within you any special understanding that grew in this time...any changes that came in you...in others...in the community as a whole.

3. If you are following this as personal exercise, journal any thoughts that have come to you. If you are sharing as a group, take time now to offer your reflections and to listen prayerfully to what each person has to say.

4. Close with a time of thanksgiving for any ways that you see community being deepened through time and with prayer that you may continue to be open to the element of time in the life you share together.

The Inner Church—A Thanksgiving
(*personal thanksgiving and awareness*)

A simple adaptation noted at the conclusion of the exercise indicates the possibility for its use in a setting of communal sharing and prayer.

1. Ask that you may let come into your mind the names or faces of any special persons who nurtured your faith in the past and still nurture you within. You may be given one or two special persons to focus on right now. It may be that a number will arise within.

2. Take time to reflect more closely on the goodness of any who have come into your awareness. What did this person/these persons give to you? What do you see that still teaches or encourages you?

3. Express your thanksgiving for any inner nurturers who have come in this time of reflection. Offer your thanksgiving to God and to them.

If a group is sharing in this exercise, let a leader gently suggest the three movements, announcing them and allowing five to six minutes for each. When the third movement is complete, invite all wishing to do so to share one person who is a vital part of their inner church.

Meditation and Thanksgiving While Engaged in a Common Task (*group*)

1. Let the leader invite all to reflect quietly on the question, "What gifts am I seeing in others that I am thankful for?" After the time of reflection, ask persons to say in a single word the gifts they have seen: "I am thankful for...." The focus here is to remain on the gifts within the group. At this point gifts, rather than names, are shared.

2. Invite all now to reflect on the question, "What am I learning as I work with others on this task?" After a time of quietness, invite all who wish to say as part of a prayer: "I am thankful for learning...."

3. Invite participants now to consider anything they are learning about one another that has nothing to do with the task itself. Take time in silence to reflect on these learnings and to give thanks for knowing one another and for being known more closely.

4. In closing, invite group members to take hands and then each, on behalf of the whole group, to say "Thank you" for the person to his/her right: "Loving God, I thank you for Heather...Ted... Frank... Jane...."

3

Practices...

T HE HEALTH of our human bonds depends on the most elemental customs. This is true in marriage and the deepest of friendships. It is surely true in the bond of parent and child. Working relationships require the same essential customs. Do we listen? Do we honor our commitments? Do we show up on time? When we have blundered, do we say "I'm sorry" and mean it? Do we compliment and encourage? These questions point to the conventions of caring. They highlight cardinal practices in the long-term nourishment of any link between one person and another.

To ignore the practices of caring is, at best, to place a momentary stress on the bond. At worst, it is to court disaster. Forget an important anniversary? Do it once, and the lapse of memory may produce a painfully embarrassed look and an awkward moment of apology. However, if a person continues to ignore opportunities for mutual celebration, the bond will surely suffer. When a parent, after a particularly harsh day, is too tired to listen to a child, the situation may be just that: an honest fatigue. If that same parent repeatedly shuts out the young life begging for attention, the link between parent and child surely will fracture under the strain.

As I began to look back over notes from many months of observing the upwellings of Christian community, certain practices started to declare themselves. Like the basic habits of healthy human bonds, these practices appeared to be essential for community life. When present, community in Christ grew strong. When absent or treated lightly, the community weakened.

In a sense, the discovery of these practices revealed nothing new. I was raking over the rudimentary and the painfully obvious. Jesus shared these matters with his gathered community from the start. He taught these practices as fundamental to the maintenance of sound relationships.He had lived them before the community. Yet the very fact that these practices merited his attention all the more declared their importance. The obvious is often what we most easily forget or choose to ignore. The more I reflected, the more I found that the almost prosaic nature of these practices strengthened, rather than muted, the call to regard them.

The common character of the practices that I was witnessing also spoke to a concern I felt. Christian community can appear to be a grand and nearly unattainable ideal. In one important respect, this impression is proper. The concept of bearing with any body of persons long term can challenge us. And to live with others as Jesus teaches challenges our pride, our self-centered perspectives, and just about everything else about us that seems natural. It is, however, only a short step from seeing the immensity of the challenge to assuming its impossibility. "People just can't do that," we may say. "It's utterly beyond reach." Or we may harbor the gnawing sense that Christian community is beyond hope for the particular group in which we find ourselves. Perhaps it is attainable for elite folk in special settings. Perhaps it exists somewhere, but not where we are. Genuine Christian community seems too lofty, too distant for us and our crowd.

The distance of Christian community tugged in the back of my mind one night when I attended a dance recital put on by students at a college not far from our home. It was an informal program. Those of us in the audience gathered in a large circle on folding metal chairs. The hardwood dance floor glistened between us. We didn't dare set a foot on it. The floor was for those who knew what they were doing. We hunched forward on our chairs and waited.

At length a young man in magnificent physical shape came out and performed a stunning solo. He leaped, froze, twirled over the entire floor. He paused when least expected, glided, cut figure after figure before our eyes, and then stopped suddenly—just as everyone yearned for more. For the second dance, a troop of five women slowly, slowly took the floor. For twenty minutes they passed before us with the subtlest of movements. Their gestures were almost imperceptible, yet the five were ever advancing, stretching, pulling our eyes in new directions. At the end, they left the circle as quietly as they had come. The third dance was a jazz solo, as sensuous as the first had been energetic and the second mysterious.

The fourth and final dance began with no one in the

circle. Old pop tunes crackled over the sound system. The young woman next to me began to inch awkwardly into the sacred space. Four others around the edges did the same. They met in the middle, laughing in pantomime. If they had dancers' bodies, they managed to conceal these under baggy jeans and old sweatshirts. They looked...well, like the rest of us. They gestured tentatively toward one another, scratched one another's heads, held hands, and then slowly began a circle dance which, over the next several minutes, grew wildly exuberant. Suddenly one of them grabbed a member of the audience and dragged her out onto the floor. Another did the same. Then one grabbed me! Now the young and the old, the stout and the straight, an ever-growing number of us, cut our own forms, made our own circles and fast moving lines. When the music stopped we stumbled back to our chairs, wheezing and cheering. We had been where we thought we could not go.

I drove home that night, my mind spinning with the goodness of the evening. The seemingly remote place of joy was not remote at all; the sacred space was not closed.

And as for the thoughts that tugged at me earlier in the evening, did I now have an answer? *Is the goodness of community in Christ really that far removed from possibility?* In Jesus' day, yes, there were elite and distant bands of community: priests, Temple scholars who knew the law like nobody's business, Essenes who lived with an austerity that still commands our wonder. But when Jesus set out to form community, there was nothing elite about it. He took common, ordinary folk and yanked them from the side. He taught them the movements, gave them the practices. The practices demanded much and challenged much. But the commonness of these practices now seems to proclaim how near are the possibilities for community in the One who draws us into the sacred space of being together.

PRAYER FOR ONE ANOTHER

My year of watching intentionally for Christian community confirmed something that had long hovered in the back of my mind. Perhaps the matter had seemed so obvious as to merit little attention. Now it pressed itself upon me in ways that declared an elemental significance. Sometimes it spoke by its presence. At other times it cried out through its absence. What I saw was simply this: The steady practice of prayer for one another is a source of immeasurable wholeness and blessing in the community of faith.

From the start Jesus modeled this practice for his community of followers. He prayed that Peter's faith not fail him (Luke 22:31-32). He prayed for unity among his disciples and sought protection for them in the midst of an unknowing and unsympathetic world (John 17). James called community members to intercede for the sick in their midst (James 5:14). Paul, in marvelously poetic words, told the Ephesians of his earnest prayer that they be filled with the very fullness of God (3:14-19). And, showing the need for a mutuality of prayer in the community of faith, Paul just as earnestly elicited the petitions of others on his own behalf (2 Thess. 3:1-2). In the Christian community, the interweaving of lives through prayer has been present from the beginning.

When we pray for another in the community of faith, we do far more than just offer our personal concerns. We enter upon what Douglas Steere has termed God's "siege of love."[1] The words of Psalm 121:4 hint at God's perpetual intercession for us: "He who keeps Israel will neither slumber nor sleep." God yearns over us with a yearning that does not stop. The divine care never ceases. And when we pray for another, we come into the realm where already we are lovingly held together. On a level deeper than words, we join with the care that surrounds us all.

In this context, even the simplest prayer for another becomes an occasion for communal formation. We offer to God our deepest desire for this one in her grief. We earnestly lift another in his cancer. We ask blessing for yet another embarking on a new venture in life. Over such elemental matters we extend the longings of our hearts. And even before the prayer has fully left us, God has drawn us yet nearer to one another.

And with our prayerfully shared longings, God forms our community through time. Our prayers for one another are part of an unfolding process. Through both joy and anguish, they are, in essence, our dialogue with God. We offer up the yearnings of our love and then wait on the loving God's response. And whatever that response may be—even if it means more waiting for us, even if it entails more wondering and pain—as we continue in the dialogue of prayer, we move closer to one another and to the One who, in the mystery, sustains and leads us forth.

For any of this to occur at all, the practice of praying for one another involves us in the most down-to-earth and practical steps. Persons keep lists. Prayer groups meet to do one thing alone: pray. Names pass over telephone lines and pump out through E-mail. Personal needs are offered to the whole community as it gathers in worship. Or a sensitive member of the community may do what I saw not long ago. After one man had shared harsh, personal pain with a group, another went over, placed a hand on his arm and quietly said, "I will be your intercessor." By such simple and daring acts the practice of praying for one another becomes real. So too, through its steady exercise, does the deepening of the bonds we share.

HONEST SPEAKING

The practice of honest speaking in the community of faith is the habit of saying what is truly on the heart. It means being straightforward with one another. It means offering necessary correction. It means sharing differences rather than hiding them. It calls for speaking face-to-face rather than behind the back. Little can do more to weaken a community of faith than the absence of direct, honest speech. And little can do more to strengthen it than the steady, sometimes painful, custom of being wholly forthright in our words with one another.

From the beginning Jesus pointed his followers toward honest speech:

> "So when you are offering your gift at the altar, if you remember that your brother or sister has something against you, leave your gift there before the altar and go; first be reconciled to your brother or sister, and then come and offer your gift" (Matt. 5:23-24).

Don't sweep the hurt aside. Don't pretend all is in order.

Face the matter and each other in order to approach God freely and unencumbered. And "if another member of the church sins against you," Jesus counseled, "go and point out the fault when the two of you are alone" (Matt.18:15). Jesus clearly called for candor.

Paul offered identical counsel to fledgling communities of faith. Members were to speak the truth in love in order that all might grow in their bonds with one another and with Christ (Eph. 4:15-16). When one in the community erred, the community was to be kind, but it also was to act. "My friends, if anyone is detected in a transgression, you who have received the Spirit should restore such a one in a spirit of gentleness" (Gal. 6:1).

This scriptural guidance we receive on all of this is clear, yet when it comes to honest speaking within the community of faith, I find an immense shyness. And I find it first within myself. If I have a difference with another, ignoring it can seem so much easier than addressing it. *Better*, I tell myself, *to talk about something else. Everyone will be more comfortable if I just let it go. And if another in the community needs correction, well, who am I to come forward with the difficult words? No. Just leave the matter alone. After all, I don't want to stir up trouble.*

The down side of this approach is that silence yields its own form of trouble. The unaddressed hurt will not go away; it only goes deeper. A genuine difference left unexplored can solidify into a hidden barrier; people will repeatedly butt into it when they try to talk of other matters. I am not the only person who has seen a community of faith suddenly explode, knowing full well that the explosion had been building for years. Amid mounting pain, people never found the graced channels for sharing what they thought. And even where there is no overt explosion, the tension of unresolved differences still can stifle community life. Without the practice of honest speech, wounds remain thinly covered and untreated. Without honest speech, the community does not open to the healing presence of the Loving One who, from the start, called it into being.

Ultimately honest speaking in the community of faith opens us to the healing presence of Christ. Honest speaking lets us set out matters that need to be shared among us. It lets us address items together which, for the health of all, we cannot put aside.

Prayer, spoken or felt deeply in silence, is essential in this process. When at last I dare to offer honest speech, I cannot speak difficult words to another without leaning on the Spirit. I do not have the wisdom to express well what I long to express, nor do I have the courage and the gentleness. And when others have spoken to me, or when I have seen them share honestly and compassionately with others, again it is the steady undergirding of prayerfulness that has lifted their words and guided them.

In the community of faith, the practice of honest speech moves far beyond "telling it like it is." It allows us to enter the places of deepest caring for one another and for the life we share. Prayerfully undertaken, it permits the Living Christ to form us on levels deeper and more whole than our reticence to speak will ever allow.

⇥⇤

I had lost my temper completely with him that afternoon. As my words poured forth, all I could see was the need to stick up for myself. Immediately after my outburst, he responded in a way I will never forget. He placed a hand on my shoulder. He paused and looked straight at me. I believe he was, in some way, praying. He then spoke words that I am sure were difficult for him: "Steve, you must learn not to take everything so personally." He put his hand down, smiled, and thinking it best that I be alone, walked away. He had dared to say what I most needed to hear. For both of us, that moment was a gift in the presence of Christ. It remains with me as a sign of the caring, honest speech God seeks in all our bonds.

ENCOURAGEMENT

A friend of mine who holds a difficult post in his denomination keeps a folder in the lower right-hand drawer of his desk. The folder contains notes, cards, and E-mail messages he has received over the years. Some of these offer words of thanks. Others extend congratulations on former accomplishments or brief words of cheer on a small number of the countless tasks that have called forth his prodigious energy. My friend hangs on to these paper trophies not out of vanity but out of practicality. "When things get rough, I take out the folder and read a few messages. It helps. I call it my 'encouragement file.'"

Encouragement is vital in the community of faith. It can uplift us in the midst of difficult work, cheer us when we feel alone, inspire us when we wonder if we are up to the task at hand. In times of distress, encouragement can come as a deep remedy for our pain.

I am not writing here about the encouragement that

comes with syrupy words and perhaps a smile but with little genuine feeling. Most of us have experienced such and, if we are honest about it, have probably offered it as well. Encouragement in Christ arises from the heart. It is prayerfully given, sometimes with many words but more often, I suspect, with few. From time to time it is given with just a glance or a touch on the arm. And whether the encouragement is offered one-on-one or poured forth in a larger gathering, it invariably builds up the whole body.

Sister Barbara Fiand has given much time to strengthening the life of Roman Catholic religious communities. To communities that are seeking practical ways to deepen their bonds, she offers this counsel: "Perhaps at the next mid-year or end-of-the-year evaluation we could resist discussing either the group's or, for that matter, any individual's failures or successes but concentrate instead on each other's gifts."[2]

Put aside all the anxious questions about how we are doing. Instead, Fiand urges that we view our common life from a different angle. Look at the talents already present. Name them to one another. Speak personally about what we see. Pause to rejoice over what we find. Perform these simple tasks, and give thanks. In our goal-driven culture, such an exercise may seem to be an ineffectual diversion. However, I have seen people follow this practice and have shared in its use. Invariably the encouragement that comes forth blesses the entire group.

Some persons clearly possess the gift of encouragement. A few of these good souls inhabit nearly every parish I have known. They write the notes and speak the words of appreciation. They manage to name our particular gifts perhaps before we have recognized them ourselves.

As I have watched congregations, I have concluded that these natural encouragers are not meant to stand in isolation. They are a sign of all we need to become. The faith community that lets just a few carry out the works of encouragement will never enjoy encouragement as a communal gift. The spirit of encouragement will move along its edges but will never exist at its core. Conversely, the faith community where all learn to follow the ways of mutual upbuilding will come to live from a love ripening at its center.

For most of us, learning the practice of encouragement comes down to a series of questions: Have I stepped across the aisle or across the room to speak the words of appreciation I feel? Have I offered the look of understanding that I wish to convey? Am I listening in a way that will encourage another's search? Am I offering others the support I need myself?

Encouragement takes effort and discipline. Personally and in the community as a whole, we need to grow in our sensitivity and our habits of mutual support. This, of course, is a lifetime task; but to the degree that we follow the practice of encouragement, we shall be heeding that so essential counsel to "outdo one another in showing honor" (Rom. 12:10). We shall be patterning ourselves after Jesus, who ceaselessly encouraged his followers so that together they might become a sign of his upbuilding presence in the world.

BEING PRESENT

The practice of being present is a gift we give to others in the community of faith. It fulfills our commitment to be there for each person and for the body as a whole no matter what the circumstances. It is rooted in an inner determination to attend on needs that arise for our sisters and brothers in Christ. It treats time with the community not as an option but as an essential in the ongoing journey of faith. The practice of being present manifests itself in steady acts of coming together, spontaneous moments of quietly drawing near, and whole days of joining life to life in the midst of the turmoil and the business that surround us.

Being present is, by its very nature, an exacting practice. Perhaps for that reason its abandonment has, from the earliest days, been an all too solid reality. The writer of the Letter to the Hebrews noted that "neglecting to meet together" (10:25) had become the habit of some. Words like "I'm too busy to go to worship" or "I just don't have time to listen right now" or "I can get by without being involved with the others" clearly predate our contemporary anxieties over weak commitment in the family of faith. The discipline of presence has always issued strong and steady demands. The temptation to drift into less rigorous ways has been around for a long time.

The existence of community depends upon the practice of being present with one another. If we do not draw together, no fresh fields of understanding will grow among us. Ties will not deepen. Bonds will not form. It is sad, but wholly understandable, that some of the bitterest expressions of disappointment with

Christian community arise where the practice of being present has thinned to the point of evaporation.

Beyond the basic matter of a community's survival, presence is essential for spiritual growth. In the days following Pentecost and the birth of the church, drawing together became an indispensable element of the new life in Christ. The gathered fellowship became the site of continued learning and expanding joy (Acts 2:41-47). Not many years later, Paul wrote his counsel on communal sharing: "Rejoice with those who rejoice, weep with those who weep" (Rom. 12:15). As persons drew together, they learned; their lives grew full; the entire body matured.

It was one of those awkward regional meetings where lay and clergy delegates from more than sixty congregations gathered to conduct the routine business of their denomination. The temperature outside hovered at ninety degrees. Inside it was worse. For most of the day the matter of being present for one another rested entirely on the level of some 150 souls' having said (probably in response to a minister's pained plea), "Sure, if you need somebody for that meeting, I'll… uh…go."

In the afternoon, the chair announced that the body would now receive six new pastors into its regional fellowship. Theoretically this was good news, but given the heat there weren't a lot of smiles. According to the bylaws, receiving six new ministers meant listening to six different people tell their faith stories.

So what happened as the first pastor told her story?

Nobody could ever quite say, except that people were drawn to be present in an added way. They found themselves listening intently to the fullness of her journey. And it was the same for the man who came after her, whose story was completely different. And it was this way again for the pastor after him, and the next, and on through to the final person. When the last one finished, all of us had forgotten about the heat. In the pew behind me an old gentleman spoke in low tones to his pastor: "I'm not sure I want to admit this, but I'm glad I came."

Sometimes the practice of being present happens in an instant. A lay leader of a congregation had come to be with his friend in the hospital. His friend could not talk through the tubes stretching down his throat. The efficient nurse at the desk had told him that his visit would have to be quick. He sat down and took his friend's hand. "Jake, it's good to see you." Jake looked back, eye to eye. The two sat in quietness for perhaps a minute, no more than two. Then the lay leader spoke a simple prayer for his friend. They looked at each other again. After this it was time to go. In a way that neither had expected, they both knew that their closeness would eternally outlast whatever events might lie immediately ahead.

A new congregation was forming near one end of our regional body of churches. I went there as often as I could. The sheer freshness of their fellowship excited me. *Were they*, I wondered, *rediscovering something that so many of us take for granted?* Every one of them mattered. And beyond that, the presence of every one mattered. "I just can't let myself miss," one young woman explained on my fourth time seeing her. "I find I gain so much—we all gain so much—by our being together."

The practice of being present for one another will play itself out in more ways than we shall ever be able to number. Whatever the context, whatever the immediate setting, if we follow the practice, then surely bonds will strengthen.

NAMING AND CLAIMING THE GOODNESS

Ultimately we need to make a practice of both naming and claiming the goodness of Christian community wherever that goodness arises. We need the courage to say aloud such simple things as "This time together has been a blessing" or "This sharing has been a gift; I'm grateful."

Naming and claiming the goodness of Christian community has nothing to do with self-satisfaction. The practice is light years away from vain and self-congratulatory declarations. To name and claim the goodness God gives us with one another is simply to acknowledge the richness of a gift that lies beyond our own making. It is to register with one another our joy in the miracle of community. It is to say boldly and with thankful hearts, "Look! How good this is!"

The root of this practice stretches far back in the witness of scripture:

How very good and pleasant it is
> when kindred live together in unity!
It is like the precious oil on the head,
> running down upon the beard,
on the beard of Aaron,
> running down over the collar of his robes.
It is like the dew of Hermon,
> which falls on the mountains of Zion.
For there the Lord has ordained his blessing,
> life forevermore.
>
> —Psalm 133

For the psalmist, the moment of community was nothing less than a place of eternal blessing, and the psalmist stated this forthrightly. To declare the blessing was to hold it at the center of one's being.

Similarly Paul, in addressing the earliest churches, named the goodness he saw and thankfully claimed it. He poured forth gratitude for wholeness when it grew among the members of the community (1 Cor. 1:4-7). He joyfully declared that by grace the community members were becoming God's field and God's building (1 Cor. 3:9), letters from Christ (2 Cor. 3:3), and ambassadors of reconciliation (2 Cor. 5:20).

Like any practice, the practice of naming and claiming the goodness of community takes time. We must pause within ourselves and with each other. We must speak openly of what we see. And, without rushing the matter, we need to give thanks.

Whatever the momentary demands, though, I have seen entire groups take exactly these steps. Some groups have been small, just five or six persons. Others have been larger: church boards with responsibility for a congregation, regional leaders and staff with responsibilities to many faith communities. Where most fruitful, the practice is a regular, disciplined part of what these groups do: "What have we seen? What blessings can we name? Let us give thanks." The ongoing process results not in self-congratulation and pride but in quiet humility and a growing awareness of gifts that nourish all.

REFLECTION AND MEDITATION

1. Where have you experienced blessing because others followed any of the practices mentioned here: prayer for one another...honest speaking...encouragement...being present...naming and claiming the goodness?

2. Where have you known blessing in community because you followed any of these practices?

3. What do you believe has helped others or yourself to observe these practices? What has hindered?

4. What practices would you add to the list offered in this chapter? How have you seen these practices strengthen and bless the community of faith?

PRAYERFUL EXERCISES

A Covenant of Practice (*personal or group*)

Make a covenant to keep one or more of the following practices for a period of four to six months. Resist any tendency to say, "I'll do all five!" If we seek communal deepening, God will draw us there more through the careful, steady focus of our energies than through our own zeal to do all things at once. If you are following some of these practices already, consider one where you sense a call to fresh growth.

1. *Pray for one another.* Commit to pray daily by name for others in the community of faith. This does not preclude the need to pray earnestly over needs beyond the community, but some communities may neglect the lives of those close at hand. So offer daily intercessions and thanksgivings for others of the fellowship.

2. *Honest speaking.* Examine where you need to be more open with others in the community of faith. Seek God's guidance that you may find the right words to say. As time passes and you grow in this practice, note what it is doing within you and in the relationships you share.

3. *Encouragement.* Make a regular discipline of encouraging others. If you send one note a week or make one call or simply speak your encouragement directly to someone else once a week, in four months you will have reached out at least seventeen times. As the weeks pass, it may be helpful to note the rich variety of situations in which encouragement can uplift lives and deepen the bonds we share in Christ.

4. *Being present.* Consider prayerfully where you can make a commitment to be more present to the community of faith than you are right now. You may find yourself drawn toward a greater presence in structured situations, such as worship or a study group or meetings. You may be led toward an

expansion of the time you spend with others in their need or into a greater openness to spontaneous opportunities for presence that arise in the life of your faith community.

5. *Naming and claiming the goodness.* After times of goodness in your community of faith, discipline yourself to speak of them to yourself, to others, and to God in thanksgiving. Such times of goodness may flow from major events; they may emerge from simple exchanges of one person with another.

A Covenant of Practice is just that: a commitment to observe regularly the simple patterns through which God graciously strengthens and intertwines our lives. If you are following a Covenant of Practice as an individual, take time at least once a month to reflect prayerfully on your learnings. If a group follows this exercise, arrange to meet once a month to share experiences and insights.

4

Blocks...

I NEVER THOUGHT I would get tired of the life at our church, but I guess that's what happened. I kept saying yes to invitations to serve on this group and on that. A bunch of us were doing more and more. For a while it really seemed exciting. Then somewhere along the line, I wore out. I think a lot of us did. I'm not sure when it happened, but we began to feel like we were being used; and then we got all used up."

The young woman had recently joined the church and was excited when a senior member of the congregation invited her to attend a small group for prayer and fellowship. After her first meeting, though, she was puzzled. The group seemed to spend so much time talking negatively about the views of people who were not present. This happened on her second visit and on her third. Then she stopped going. "I just didn't find what I needed," she said. "There was a certain closeness among the people, but it didn't feel good. I'm not sure it felt good to them either. They didn't seem all that happy."

Three ministers sharing their weekly Monday morning coffee together half laughed, half grumbled when they realized that the three denominations they represented had managed to reorganize themselves seven times in the last twelve years, and two of the denominations were about to do it again. "It sure keeps us from having time to look one another in the eye," one of them ventured. The others nodded. A little later they parted for the week, grateful for the coffee fellowship and aching over the continued decline of closeness in their denominational bodies.

It was Youth Sunday, and some of the adults nervously awaited what they might hear from the pulpit. Seventeen-year-old John more than justified their apprehensions. He delivered a simple rhetorical question with all the brashness of youth and a wholly genuine smile. Two-thirds of the congregation groaned inside when he asked it; the remaining third cheered silently; one uninhibited lady of eighty-three lifted her right hand high in the air and give a thumbs up. "Don't you think," he asked, "that we could build our shared life here on our joy in Christ rather than on our perpetual debates over what color carpet to use in the lounge?"

More often than we care to admit, Christian community can run dry. Fellowship shrivels and grows hard.

The once fresh realms of coming together grow stale. Where persons formerly tendered nourishment for one another's souls, now little feeding takes place; and the community as a whole has only sparse offerings for hungers of the spirit. In such a place, once strong patterns of commitment yield to disengagement. Both numerically and spiritually, the community dwindles.

Or the decline may not be outward. It may be more a case of missing the mark from the start. The community never really demonstrates the love it proclaims. Whether a small group or a large body, it disappoints those who come seeking. The community may have a certain form of closeness, but to the sensitive "it doesn't feel good."

Or some debilitating weakness may constrict the life of a potentially healthy community. In many ways the community may be strong. It may reach out to others with exciting programs. Many of its members may engage in selfless acts of love. Yet something hinders its ability to be the vibrant body it really can be. Distractions lay hold and tie it down. Time and energy flow into efforts that do not advance the reign of God's love. In the end, devout participants sense a shackling of the life they share together. And even the most realistic members, those who understand that no community in Christ will ever be perfect, feel a sadness for what they are missing.

I would venture that all of us who have rejoiced in the blessings of Christian community have also grieved over its failure. We have seen community grow weak. Many of us have experienced the sting of its absence, the lingering pain of its loss, or the ache of its unfulfilled possibilities. We may have watched while a community of faith we loved slowly went dry. When any of this occurs, questions arise within us: Why has this happened? What has thwarted the goodness? What is impeding the love that once flowed?

Such questions have no easy answers and may tempt us to abide in the sadness. Abide in the sadness, or fix blame: "If only Florence...Bob...Cindy...weren't a part of this group." The stifling of community in Christ is indeed sad, and surely individual actions can negatively affect a community. Yet I am increasingly convinced that certain major blocks to community life are themselves communal in nature. These blocks can frustrate and deeply harm our life in community.

The blocks may arise from within the community, or the community may adopt them from the culture in which it finds itself. Either way, they are all the more effective because they become a part of the way we live. We do not intentionally weaken the community. Nevertheless, if we tolerate the blocks through time, they sap our common strength. If we carry them about long enough, we may shape them into our own self-constructed barriers.

In mentioning the blocks that follow, I confess I have contributed my full share to their enhancement. I confess too that I do not know the full dimensions of these blocks nor of others that we set up among us. Even so, I have selected these four blocks in particular because of their prevalence in our contemporary communities of faith. And I mention them because only as we name them clearly shall we seek the grace we need to set them aside.

FATIGUE

Not long ago a friend of mine related how, over the period of a few years, he witnessed the decline of a fine retreat center. A staff small in number but rich in the gifts of hospitality ran the center. Every spring my friend and several others journeyed there for a three-day retreat. Part of the time they would pass in quietness, part of it in shared reflection and worship. Invariably they returned to their homes and places of work refreshed.

The change was subtle at first. More groups began to use the facility, which was fine. The spacious grounds and more than adequate sleeping quarters allowed for that growth. Then one spring the staff responsible for the center grew by one: a business and marketing manager. In the next two years, usage increased dramatically—still with no overcrowding problems. Working under added pressure, though, the staff became less gracious. Simple questions that used to receive smiles and thoughtful responses now drew curt answers. Tension permeated the once relaxed atmosphere. Hospitality, long the hallmark of that small receiving community, had fled. Eventually my friend's group looked for another place to hold its spring retreat.

My friend regarded this transition with sadness. Because the community had overextended itself, it had lost the very gift it was seeking to share. "It's sad too," my friend said, "because I know that communities I have been a part of have done the same thing. We try too hard. We wear ourselves out."

My friend saw the situation as a well-focused parable, and in this I believe he was wholly right. In the community of faith, exhaustion often claims far more than just an isolated individual here and there. It can extend to the body as a whole. Trying too hard, we collectively lose the graces we yearn to offer. Expecting more of ourselves than God does and anticipating less of God than we ought, we dull our witness to Christ's love rather than allow it to shine more brightly. This is so not just for parishes and congregations but for denominational boards, church committees, seminaries, even groups that gather to address highly specific human needs in the name of Christ.

The motives that propel us toward exhaustion are thoroughly plausible. Were they not, we would act on them with less zest. We may, with the best of intentions, be seeking to preserve something we know is good. We may feel the total burden of some cause to which we are giving our best collective energy. Or we hear the litany that begins, "Why doesn't the church…?" and feel constrained to respond at every point. "Why doesn't the church take over training the unemployed? do a better job of teaching sexuality? do more to house the homeless? develop environmental resource packets? do more for the young? do more for the elderly? share Christ with the perpetrators of crime? share Christ with the victims of crime?" and on and on. All of these are worthwhile concerns. Can we turn our back on any of them? If we try to focus our energies and trim the list, guilt can wound us.

And yet however worthy our motivations, the yield of our overextension is bleak and unfulfilling. "Are grapes gathered from thorns, or figs from thistles?" Jesus asked (Matt. 7:16). Drawing on little more than our own anxiety, we try too much and grow dispirited.

Energies deplete. Strength drains away. Nonstop earnestness bears fruit in ebbing patience and meetings that run too long. Weary, we grow all the more frightened of the future. I have too often seen, and too often now been a part of, communities where our self-nurtured fatigue led us not toward our dreams but into a nonproductive crabbiness.

There are divinely given paths that would lead us around the block of our fatigue. John Mogabgab has pointed out that Jesus' invitation to his disciples to come away and rest for a while arose not at the conclusion of their work but when they were so busy "they had no leisure even to eat" (Mark 6:31).[1] As communities of faith, we are discovering that sabbath rest beckons not as a distraction but as an essential element in our life together and in our witness to a weary world. In chapter 6 of this book we will look at some of the channels for the steady renewal of our corporate life. At this point, however, I would invite us to tarry over the block of fatigue itself. We need once again to name it and to see clearly its sad and thwarting power among us.

BRITTLENESS

Brittle faith is a faith that allows scant flexibility for others' honest search. Fragile, it expresses discomfort with experiences that differ from its own. Delicate, it braces itself with firmly set answers even when other deeply devoted and faithful persons gently suggest that matters may not be as simple as they appear. Often defensive, brittle faith spends much of its time judging others as being unworthy and unfaithful.

Brittleness is the sole possession neither of the

theological left nor the theological right. I once attended a four-day conference on Community in Christ. On the third day an older gentleman stood up, acknowledged that he was quite conservative and that persons of his persuasion had at times been harsh in shutting out the views of others. He then went on to suggest that others of more liberal views had perhaps done the same. Instantly a pastor was on his feet, his face red with anger. "That's absolutely not true of us liberals!" he said. "All the narrowness is on your side!"

I ached in that moment partly because the second speaker represented much of what I would stand for. I ached mainly, though, because the red face and accusatory response verified the point the man sought so vehemently to deny. Brittleness and the defensive anger it spawns reflect the failings of no single part of the body. They are available to us all.

The outcroppings of brittleness often occur in the minute and the personal. A pastor tries to meet the needs of some of her folk through modest additions to a Sunday service and receives hate mail from others who are threatened by the mild changes. A man expresses his honest quest for images of God that will touch him within and is plainly told by a long-standing member of the community, "What you are doing is crap." I have seen, alas, all too many situations like these. When brittle faith snaps, its edges are razor sharp. Its wounds are deep.

If brittleness spreads widely, it can divide and impoverish the faith community as a whole. Persons will judge ideas before fully hearing and understanding them. New thoughts and fresh ways of expressing the divine mystery will be turned aside as threat. Similarly, dearly cherished and deeply meaningful older ways may, by the brittleness of others, be too swiftly dismissed. In the end, the whole community grows weak.

Jesus clearly pointed the community of faith away from all brittleness. One day his disciples approached him about a man they encountered who was casting out demons (Mark 9:38-40). The man was doing good work, but "we tried to stop him, because he was not following us." He wasn't fully in step. He probably didn't know all the lore. The man may have looked a little different and maybe even spoke in slightly altered phrases. "Don't do it!" they had told him. Jesus, in response, set the brittleness aside: "Whoever is not against us is for us." Let him be. Look deeply. Be flexible now. See, I'm working through him too.

Scripture as a whole consistently softens the brittle boundaries we erect so swiftly. In the Book of Ruth an alien woman becomes a paradigm of faith. The parable of the Good Samaritan places an alien man in the same role. The Book of Jonah stands as an everlasting monument against narrow visions of God's mercies. Inveighing against old barriers, Colossians states, "There is no longer Greek and Jew, circumcised and uncircumcised, barbarian, Scythian, slave and free; but Christ is all and in all!" (3:11). Living faith dissolves the brittle barriers that block community. It counsels, "Don't be afraid. See the breadth of God's work among you!"

And yet for all the steady witness of scripture, brittleness continues as a major impediment in our shared life. It lies at the root of many of the internal divisions

Great Scripture

Great Scripture

currently fracturing our various communions and denominations. It still exerts its age-old power to keep us apart in the very places where the Living Christ would free us for deeper sharing.

LOSS OF FOUNDATION

I have never seen a community of faith intentionally abandon its foundation in Christ Jesus. Thinking back over the years, I cannot point to a single community that said, "Here now, let us withdraw from the One who called us into being." I have sat through more church meetings than I can number and never have I heard a lay leader or pastor say, "We shall fill our minds with distractions and thus have less time to live on deeper levels where the Loving One seeks to draw us together." Such a statement would sound absurd to speaker and hearer alike.

And yet it happens. Distractions mount. Energies flow in ways that allow primal bonds to weaken. Roots detach. Disengaged from its source, the community loses its aim. And even if the community does not fully recognize its own plight, it lives intimately with the symptoms: the departure of common joy, anxiety concerning the future, a deep wondering over *Why are we here anyway?*

I am still discomforted by the experience a young man related over lunch not long after I began to inquire more intently about the presence of community in Christ. "Where have you seen it?" I asked. My tone was too bright, my words too quick for the reality he had known. He hesitated and then asked tentatively, "Can I speak of Christian community's darker side?"

Over the next hour he told of a community gone awry. In many respects, it was a familiar story. Founded in love, the community somewhere became preoccupied with smaller matters: what color to paint a hallway, what fabric to put on the pews, what tune to use for singing praise as the offering was brought forth. "These may have been important items," he said, "but they were not worth the endless going back and forth, week after week after week."

The young man and his wife had come to the community with a deep and open need. Though they were patient and undemanding, their distress grew as time passed, and they received no support whatsoever for their situation. Ultimately they got caught between two sides in a needless dispute. Deeply hurt, they withdrew. "In the end," he said, "all we could find there was a lot of activity on things that didn't matter that much."

We do not forsake the foundation of our common life just for the small and the particular. About the time of my ordination thirty years ago, large portions of the church had come to admire the success of secular ventures, particularly those undertaken in the commercial world. Management By Objective became our channel into a brighter future for the family of faith. We spent whole meetings stuffing into our minds the difference between a goal and an objective. I recall a cluster of us gathering one Saturday to learn something called "Pair Weighing," a process touted as a builder of bonds and a clarifier of direction. At the conclusion of the day we went forth to shower this new tool like manna throughout the churches of our region.

In this endeavor we possessed the best intentions.

We were latching onto something that seemed so large and important. Unknown to us, we also were neglecting weightier matters on which the health of our communities depended. I finally got to use Pair Weighing to help a group decide where, with the least conflict, they could cut back their support of others in need.

In our communities we sometimes shun the more rigorous demands of faith for the easier diversions of a shallow sociability. We may become mired in procedural issues, get caught up in power politics, or allow the least important matters to become primary. So doing, we cut ourselves off from the essentials of love and devotion. We allow a pervasive film of distraction to grow between us and the One who seeks to be at the foundation of all we do.

We may respond to this primary loss with declarations that we believe will take care of the matter: "We have forgotten what we are about!" "We need to get back to the basics!" While such statements can be wholly true, by themselves they are not enough. With regard to the loss of foundation, what we most need right now is a thoughtful and painful pausing. Before we speak too swiftly the cure, will we dare ask to see the extent of the malady? Will we venture to pray that we spot even the smallest instances where we start to draw our life from something other and infinitely less than the Source of all our life together?

DESPAIR

Despair in our common life comes as a sadness that claims, "What we once had together in Christ is lost. It cannot come back again." Despair is the melancholy that lets people look on the troubles of their community and then conclude that little hope exists for any future form of community in any place. Despair pessimistically says, "Decay will only continue" and then, having said this, does not lift its eyes to search for fresh possibilities. As an impediment to community, despair can be all encompassing and utterly lethal.

Despair over our common life is among the most hidden of blocks. For the most part we do not like to air our distress. We fear that our own sadness might draw others down. So holding our disappointments within, we find that our burden grows heavier. Given the hiddenness of despair, I was not surprised when, in one week's time, three devoted leaders took me to the side in different settings and confided their near hopelessness for the future of the community they had loved for so long. One wept as he spoke.

Despair can issue, hard and fully formed, from the other blocks. Amid fatigue, it may suddenly erupt. Where brittleness slices communal bonds, despair can seal off all hope of reconciliation. And where community life separates from its foundation, despair can thwart even the most ardent hopes of resting on that foundation again.

Despair is also a result of the current, widespread propensity for focusing on the negative. In the community of faith, as in the culture around us, often our minds are more attuned to what is wrong than to the subtle movements of grace. We easily name the failures. They are rock solid and before us. When we see a goodness, will we risk speaking of it or, we wonder, would we sound hopelessly naive in doing so? If hope tugs within us for a moment, will we take it seriously or should we swiftly set our hope aside as mere sentimentality? Without even pausing to answer such questions, we may find ourselves drawn back to matters that only deepen our pessimism.

If the movements of despondency often are quiet and inward, their effects nonetheless are decidedly public. In community, we seldom experience despair in isolation. This is so even if we keep silent and believe we are alone in our pain. What is felt within one nearly always moves outward to others. If persons do not openly say, "Our community is broken," the sense of brokenness still will influence the community's life.

No easy ways to counter communal despair exist, and yet the biblical record of common life offers a clear and persistent response to despair whenever it obstructs the fellowship of faith. The response, not of our own making, comes as a gift. Our task is to be aware of its presence and claim it. "Why?" wrote the prophet Isaiah to the children of Israel in a time of deep communal distress.

> Why do you say, O Jacob,
> and speak, O Israel,
> "My way is hidden from the Lord,
> and my right is disregarded by my God"?

Why are you in despair? Why have you claimed that all is now lost and that God is no longer near?

> Have you not known? Have you not heard?
> The Lord is the everlasting God,
> the Creator of the ends of the earth.
> He does not faint or grow weary;
> his understanding is unsearchable.

Don't you see? God does not stop or step aside.

> [God] gives power to the faint,
>   and strengthens the powerless.
> Even youths will faint and be weary,
>   and the young will fall exhausted;
> but those who wait for the Lord
>   shall renew their strength,
>   they shall mount up with wings like eagles,
> they shall run and not be weary,
>   they shall walk and not faint (40:27-31).

"My people," says the Lord, "all is not lost. Wait, and I shall renew."

This response to communal despair is as old as the promise of deliverance to a people crushed by slavery in Egypt. It is as fresh as the announcement made to a community shattered by its grief: "Go and tell my brothers to go to Galilee; there they will see me" (Matt. 28:10). God will not let go. God seeks to mend our brokenness, heal our bondage, make our shattered life whole.

At times the persistent note of God's care for us is hard to take in. Israel struggled for decades in the wilderness. Was God really with them? Would they find the land they sought? The community that first heard Isaiah's words needed to hear them again and again. The post-Resurrection fellowship of the early church required constant reminders of Jesus' presence through long seasons of trial and testing.

In the end we must return to the stark reality of this particular block itself and to the importance of acknowledging it. Once set in place, the wall of communal despair is exceedingly strong. Only when the community of faith allows itself to be totally claimed and greatly stretched will the wall crumble and new life burst forth.

REFLECTION AND MEDITATION

1. Of the four blocks cited in this chapter (fatigue, brittleness, loss of foundation, despair), which one have you experienced most closely? What effect did it have on you? on your community of faith?

2. What other blocks would you add to the list?

3. To what block are you most prone?

4. What has most helped you and others become aware of the blocks when they are present?

5. What do you find helpful in overcoming the blocks?

PRAYERFUL EXERCISES

Prayerful Meditation on a Block to Community Life (*personal*)

1. After a time of coming to quiet, ask that God gently lead you to see anything that is now hindering the fullness of community in the fellowship of which you are a part:...any hurtful patterns...any barriers to fullness of sharing.

2. Take time to reflect on any block that comes to mind. Write it down or name it aloud. If more than one block comes into your awareness, take time with each and then ask that now you may focus on one in

particular. Let that block come forth to you. Again name it aloud or write it down.

3. Reflect prayerfully on the effect this block is having on your faith community and on you.

4. Ask that you may see any manner in which you yourself are contributing to the presence of this block. In what ways is it impeding you? In what ways are you increasing the size of the block by your attitudes? your actions? your expectations?

5. Giving thanks for any insights that have come, pray that you may be more aware of the presence of the block in your own life and may receive the grace to grow free of it.

For use with group exploration: If a group is working together, encourage members to do this exercise individually and then share their insights and their prayers for growth with one another. The group members may wish to make a covenant to return periodically to check on one another's experiences in dealing with the blocks they have named.

Meditation, Reflection, and Prayer on Blocks to Community Life (*group*)

1. After offering an opening prayer for God's guidance, invite the group into a time of quiet reflection on the question: "What right now are the particular blocks to wholeness in our common life?"

2. Then invite the group to continue in silence, reflecting on how these blocks have come to be present in the community: How have they arisen? How aware of them is the community?

3. Invite group members to name in a single sentence or two the blocks that each has seen. After naming the blocks, allow a time of clarification. What does the group as a whole seem to be seeing? What fresh insights have come?

4. Again invite a return to silence and reflect on the question: "How can we set aside the blocks that have been named?"

5. After the time of quietness, share and discuss insights that have emerged.

6. When all insights and ideas have been shared, the group may close with a time of thanksgiving for blessings in its common life and with prayer to act on any fresh insights that have emerged in this time of prayerful exploration.

Blocks and God's Grace for Restoring Community (*group*)

Leaders and pastors often offer Isaiah 40:27-31 as a testimony to God's willingness to aid each of us in his or her times of greatest exhaustion and distress. While this personal approach to the passage is appropriate, notice that Isaiah's words were first addressed to the community as a whole. The following exercise approaches the passage with this original, communal intent in mind.

1. Noting that Isaiah first addressed the passage to the entire faith community in a time of exile and distress, read or have a group member read Isaiah 40:27-31 aloud.

2. Read verse 27 again and then invite the group to reflect in quietness: Where, right now, does our way

seem to be "hid[den] from the Lord"? Where is the community blocked, impeded, or hindered in its common life?

3. Continue after a time of quiet reflection by reading verses 28–31 again. Now invite the group to reflect in quietness, giving time to each of the following questions: Where have you seen God provide renewal for a blocked or weakened community of faith? How did that community "wait for the Lord"? What would it mean now for your community to "wait for the Lord"?

4. Let members of the group share any insights, reflections, or experiences that have come to them during the time of quiet reflection.

5. In closing, read or have a member read once more the words from Isaiah, and then the group may enter into a time of prayer, spoken and silent, over the reflections just shared and the group insights received.

JOURNALING *(personal or group)*
Awareness of a Block: Its Nature and the Nature of Responses to It

Conduct this exercise over a period of at least four weeks to create greater awareness of a particular block and of the ways to set it aside or move beyond it.

1. Let the individual or group select a particular block to community life that requires exploration and response.

2. Once a week for at least a month, let the participant(s) journal freely in response to three questions:
   - Where have I seen this block in recent days?
   - How is this block affecting our shared life?
   - What appear to be liberating responses to this block?

3. After several weeks of following the exercise, review the journal notes. Look for patterns, recurrent themes, growing insights. Reflect on these. What are they saying about the block? about responses to it?

4. Whether a group or an individual has followed this exercise, it will help to have a time of closure that includes thanksgiving for any new awareness and prayer to live more freely in community as a result of this growing awareness.

5

Stretched...

S EVERAL YEARS ago while leading a workshop on prayerful discernment, I stressed that when God speaks in our lives, God often speaks slowly, peaceably, and with emerging clarity. At the close of the workshop, a rugged gentleman of about sixty approached me as I was heading out the door. "I don't mean to be disrespectful," he said, "but isn't there more to God's speaking than just gentleness and peace? I mean, didn't Jesus tell us he came not to bring peace but a sword? Didn't he say that our foes might be those of our own household and that we would need to take up the cross?"

I sputtered an inadequate response that I no longer remember. Whatever it was, he received it in a spirit of kindness. He obviously accepted me and the bumbling effort I had made, even though his questions hung unanswered in the air between us.

In subsequent conversations I learned far more about this man and his circumstances. While he had no foes in his own household, he and his wife recently had assented to a difficult call from their wider community of faith and were now in the process of setting aside his highly successful medical practice and her work as an experienced administrator. They soon would leave for an impoverished land that greatly needed their skills. For the next several years they would be living at great distance from their grown children, grandchildren, and an aging parent. The decision had not come easily; but "for two years the matter kept popping up, and we just couldn't turn it aside."

Harkening back to that workshop on discernment, I could argue that ultimately the couple was at peace about their discernment, that indeed God had worked slowly and gently through their decision-making process. To do this, however, would be to miss the essential point that the good man tried to share with me. If we live in the community that belongs to Christ Jesus, then at times we will be greatly discomforted in our lives. We will be stretched in ways we had not anticipated at all.

Biblically, God's very first act with the community of faith was an act of stretching. We can recall God's first words to Abraham and Sarah:

> "Go from your country and your kindred and your father's house to the land that I will show you. I will make of you a great nation, and I will bless you, and make your name great, so that you will be a blessing" (Gen. 12:1-2).

Abraham, Sarah, and their offspring would be stretched to the very point of becoming a blessing for all peoples. This would happen only as they obeyed God's claim on their lives. They needed to leave everything—right now.

Jesus himself swiftly stripped any illusions of ease from potential followers:

As they were going along the road, someone said to him, "I will follow you wherever you go." And Jesus said to him, "Foxes have holes, and birds of the air have nests; but the Son of Man has nowhere to lay his head." To another he said, "Follow me." But he said, "Lord, first let me go and bury my father." But Jesus said to him, "Let the dead bury their own dead; but as for you, go and proclaim the kingdom of God." Another said, "I will follow you, Lord; but let me first say farewell to those at my home." Jesus said to him, "No one who puts a hand to the plow and looks back is fit for the kingdom of God" (Luke 9:57-62).

Such words still grate in our ears, and they should. From the start, Jesus made the matter clear. To join the fellowship of his people was to walk the paths of uncertainty. To say "yes" to his invitation was to unite with a company that he would persistently draw into new, often troublesome realms.

The community of Jesus is patently the community of the stretched: stretched by him, stretched for him, and stretched to be a blessing to others. Echoing the words spoken by God to Abraham and Sarah, the First Letter of Peter declared to the early church:

But you are a chosen race, a royal priesthood, a holy nation, God's own people, in order that you may proclaim the mighty acts of him who called you out of darkness into his marvelous light.

Once you were not a people,
    but now you are God's people;
once you had not received mercy,
    but now you have received mercy (2:9-10).

The letter breaks into poetry with the fullness of what is

happening, and we wonder, *Dare we grow into what is being announced? Can we let ourselves be drawn into the new life? Can we both receive and relay God's new way?*

In my mind I frequently catch a particular echo of all this. Perhaps it is because as I grow older I am more aware of the terrible daring that must have been involved. In 1939, despite severe threats from the Nazis, the confessing Christians of Germany declared that Christ alone was Head of the church and that the church

> has to testify in the midst of a sinful world, with its faith as with its obedience, with its message as with its order, that it is solely [Christ's] property, and that it lives and wants to live solely from his comfort and his direction in the expectation of his appearance.[1]

Those who signed this document paid dearly: exile and execution in Nazi death camps. As a community and with their lives, they stated the persistent truth: A Christian community becomes fully such when it dares to live from Christ alone.

If our own forms of being stretched are far humbler, I nonetheless am increasingly surprised by how often "being stretched" is a part of life in the communities I see. To say this is not to affirm that we are as fully stretched in our contemporary communities of faith as Christ would have us. It is, however, to acknowledge that his action on us is ceaseless. If we claim his name for our community, then even if it is in a weakened state, even if our community diverts its energies into the ways of faithlessness, he will tug persistently at the edges of our common life. We can ignore him. We can fail to respond. But he will not quit.

FOR OTHERS

If a man of sixty reminded me that Jesus speaks to his community through times of discomfort and stretching, a teenager and his mother focused the matter even more sharply. The woman told me over coffee that while they were on vacation she and her family had looked in the yellow pages one Sunday for a place to worship. They spotted an eye-catching announcement and decided to attend that particular church.

"The music was contemporary" she said, "and wonderfully played. The mood of the service was positive. The songs were uplifting, the readings full of hope. The sermon focused on self-esteem and reaching our life goals."

Following the model of some other rapidly expanding congregations, there was no cross to be seen in the sanctuary. But, the woman noted, the amphitheater-like seating did draw people into a kind of physical community that converged on a softly lit stage area.

Anticipating her children's delight in the experience, she asked their thoughts about the service. The eldest, a sixteen-year-old, responded with a single sentence: "You know, Mom, in there we didn't pray for anybody but ourselves."

The woman hesitated after sharing those words with me, then continued. "I've been thinking ever since that what I and my family want is to be part of a church that is living not just for ourselves but for others."

I nodded in response, and thought to myself, *Out of the mouths of the young and the open.*

In the community formed by Jesus, we are to be stretched continuously for others in their need. This has

been so from the start. When Jesus first drew his followers together, he did not turn them in upon themselves. Immediately he sent them to treat massive hurts
of spirit and body that festered in the world around
them (Matt. 10:1-8). When he spoke of the community
that would abide eternally in God's presence, it clearly
would be the community of those who fed the hungry,
welcomed the stranger, clothed the naked, cared for the
sick, visited the prisoner (Matt. 25:31-46). And when
the writer of James sought to convey to the early church
the essence of faithful living, he pointed to the practical
act of caring for widows and orphans (1:27).

In all of this I find a tremendous tension with much
of what currently passes for community both inside and
outside the church. When we say we desire community,
often we mean self-centered community: community
that will meet our needs; community that will treat our
loneliness; community that will attend on our interests
and fulfill our own burning desires.

I use the words *we* and *our* here because I am not
sure any one of us is totally free from this pattern. In
our present culture, often self is where matters begin
and end. Frequently no source of guidance emerges beyond the questions we generate about ourselves: What
will I get out of this? How will this meet my needs?
Under such standards of examination, the circle of concern narrows to a fine point. Community comes to be
evaluated not on the basis of how it connects us to the
wider human family but simply in terms of how it
relates to our self-articulated needs.

The operative word for what Christ truly asks of our
communities could easily be *obedience*. In our communi-

ties of faith, do we truly practice obedience to the One we profess to follow? Do we obey Christ as he leads us to look toward our neighbor in need? Yet the more I have seen of communities that actually let themselves be stretched for others, the more I have come to consider that *obedience* does not capture the fullness of what is happening. It embraces part of it but only part. The far more appropriate word is *vibrancy*. Wherever in Christ's name and by his love people reach out, there is life: life in the reaching community; life growing within it and moving forth; life drawn from Christ, spread abroad, and shimmering for all.

The regional gathering was immense. All the participants were women except a few of us who had been invited as guests and were received with overwhelming hospitality. They talked of social justice, but clearly they were doing a lot more than talking. Back in their home areas they taught others, wrote letters, sang songs, marched, and carried signs. Their energy now spilled over into their workshops, their meetings, their laughter, their prayers. After the gathering, on the four-hour drive back to my office, I think I smiled the whole way.

It was a small congregation. Humbly, but with much excitement, they told a group of outsiders about their growing ministry to single parents. Several of these persons, newly united to their fellowship, joined in the telling. The story was all the more striking because less than three years earlier the regional body overseeing that congregation had nearly closed its doors. The congregation had reached beyond itself, and, in the reaching, had discovered new life.

I find that these good moments and others like them bring my thoughts back to a sixteen-year-old who missed praying for other people. He knew the essential lesson. As we let the Living Christ stretch us for others, bit by bit, he broadens the tight horizons of our love, pain is eased, and we become the people he created us to be.

By Others

In Christian community we not only are stretched *for others* in their need. We are fully as much stretched *by others* whose love and faithfulness challenge our own. My sister in Christ beckons me to become more fully formed in faith than I already am. My brother in Christ invites me to grow beyond the point where I stand in my life right now. This process is sometimes subtle, sometimes dramatic. I will start with the latter if for no other reason than to share a gratitude that can never be fully expressed.

I use a small daily devotional guide that provides a scripture reading plus a description of Christians in mission. The descriptions are void of sentimentality, but they usually highlight circumstances that are immediately uplifting. I was, then, stopped short one day when the meditation told, in stark terms, of the recent martyrdom of three devout Iranian Christians. The Reverend

Mehdi Dibaj had been sentenced to die for apostasy. He was released, then arrested again and, along with another minister, was assassinated. A man who had petitioned for his release, the Reverend Haik Hovsepian, an Assemblies of God bishop, disappeared and was found dead. The meditation noted that Mr. Dibaj wrote the following as he awaited the carrying out of his death sentence:

> With greetings, I, Christian prisoner Mehdi Dibaj, Son of Hassan, with respect to the Name of God and the faith in Jesus Christ our Lord and Saviour, accept the court verdict with joy and peace.... I donate my belongings to the church and give my children into the hands of God, who is able to keep them safe so that they grow in the grace and knowledge of our Lord Jesus Christ. Amen.[2]

I have been unable to put that page of the devotional guide out of my mind. Periodically I return to it. Could I ever give so much as those three gave? Were I asked, could I show the peace and joy in Christ that shine so undeniably in Mehdi Dibaj's words?

Some evenings my wife and I play a recording of lovely, meditative songs. The back of the album cover carries the striking faces of the bishop and five North American women martyred in the struggles for justice in El Salvador during the late 1970s and early 1980s. The title of the album is *So Full of Deep Joy*. The dedication reads in part: "Their witness to total self-giving for the poor and oppressed is a gift to all of us, challenging us to live more deeply and more faithfully the Gospel word of justice, compassion and peace."[3] By such sisters and brothers in the community of faith we are ceaselessly stretched.

We are stretched as well by a large number of folk whose walk in faith, if less dramatic, still touches us deeply. I recall an underpaid truck driver and his wife. At the end of each week on the road he would arrive home with bags full of bottles and cans he had harvested from roadside picnic tables. The wife would smash the cans and sort the bottles behind their mobile home and then haul the whole rattling mess to the recycling center. Every cent they got went to feed the hungry.

We all have our lists of such people. They quietly act. They hook our attention. They teach by their deeds. Paul once counseled, "In humility regard others as better than yourselves" (Phil. 2:3). Many teachings in the Bible are hard to follow. If we will look around us, this may be among the easier.

CONFLICT

The more I see of conflict in the church, the more I am moved by persons who allow conflict to become the occasion of their growth. And wherever several persons allow personal growth to happen, their collective growth may begin to reshape the community of which they are a part. To say this is in no way to make light of the number of church and denominational conflicts that swirl about us. It is to say, though, that Jesus seeks to form us even in the places of greatest friction. In the midst of division and hurt, he can draw us toward maturity in fresh and formative ways. This formation can take place whether we happen to be the focal point of a conflict; its anguished observer; or, in some formally defined role, are present to the situation as "conflict manager."

In matters of conflict, Jesus shapes his community fundamentally by pointing it toward a healing intent. Nowhere in the Gospels does Jesus deny conflict. At no time, in his own actions or in his counsel to others, does he ignore its presence or imply that conflict itself is evil. However, Jesus unceasingly encourages his followers to reach after wholeness. Where there is dispute, do not dismiss the other; swiftly seek reconciliation (Matt. 5:21-26). If a grievance arises in the common life, deal with it face-to-face in hopes of healing (Matt. 18:15). Jesus declares that peacemakers are the "children of God" (Matt. 5:9). Knowing that his own community could fracture, on the night of his betrayal Jesus earnestly prays

> "that they may be one, as we are one, I in them and you in me, that they may become completely one, so that the world may know that you have sent me and have loved them even as you have loved me" (John 17:22-23).

The community of Jesus is to embody wholeness. By its unity others will know the presence of the living God. Jesus relentlessly presses that point.

And to put it mildly, Jesus' relentlessness is discomforting. It will not allow us to dismiss easily the fractures in our common life. If we decide to take Jesus seriously and try to address the brokenness, we may find that we are in over our heads. Should we attempt to pass the situation off as "just the way things are around here," the divisions will continue to gnaw at us, as will Jesus' persistent counsel of wholeness.

And it is precisely at the point of discomfort with this state of affairs that significant stretching is taking place in the contemporary church. Part of the stretching has to do with the growing knowledge of conflict itself, its dynamics and its potential for moving persons into places of greater insight. For nearly two decades church leaders have increasingly emphasized conflict management. At its best, this emphasis has proved to be an avenue for growing wisdom and wholeness. Skilled practitioners of the art of conflict management have been a gift to many injured communities.

Beyond the movement into conflict management itself, I have experienced two other ways in which communities of faith find themselves stretched during conflict. Each has a vital role to play not only in healing the brokenness but also in lessening the incidence of fracture itself. The two are prayer and deep listening.

Not long after accepting my present call, I attended a horribly conflicted church meeting. When matters were at their worst, the moderator of the meeting invited all into a time of silent prayer. She did this with firmness, compassion, and a sense of profound need all rolled into one. After the quietness ended, the group by no means agreed on the issue at hand. As matters proceeded, though, it was clear that the entire body had been drawn into a far more gracious and open space.

During conflict the avenues of prayer are many. I have known persons who, in the midst of searing controversy, will take time each day to pray to be cleansed of bitterness. I have seen communities come to greater wholeness after regularly acknowledging their need of healing in corporate worship. I have known small groups of persons to pause before heading into highly volatile situations and, in deep supplication, to seek God's wisdom for the difficult hours that lie ahead. Such prayers are born in humility. They spring forth when we acknowledge our brokenness and the stark inadequacy of our own efforts to cobble together reconciliation.

And in this place of humility, deep listening arises. This listening waits to hear what the Spirit may be trying to say through the other. This listening does not deny difference or force agreement but seeks to understand the needs, fears, and insights of the one speaking. It is wholly separate from the listening that tries to craft a response while the other talks or hears only in order to defend itself. It is the listening of those who take with full seriousness the counsel of James: "Let everyone be quick to listen, slow to speak" (James 1:19). It is, essentially, a gift that arises wherever persons yearn to hear the Voice that beckons beyond and through all the other voices.

I once asked a group of lay people where they had experienced their greatest growth while serving as leaders in their congregations. A woman with many years of service answered quickly, "In conflict." Her response startled a few others, but the lines of growth for her and her congregation were keenly marked. In the midst of a searing situation, she and others had been stretched: stretched by Jesus' healing intent; stretched into new understandings of conflict itself; stretched, through prayer and deep listening, into closer bonds with the One they sought to follow. Such growth had not been easy. She didn't smile when she answered the question. But the growth had been real, and in spite of one person's nervous prodding she would not take back her answer.

TOUGH QUESTIONS

Certain tough questions cut across denominational lines, and they will not go away. The nature of their toughness varies according to our perspective. They are tough for some of us because we cannot resolve them personally or within our extended faith communities. For others of us they are tough because we feel the answers are clear, and we wonder why the questions weren't settled long ago. For yet others of us, the questions are tough because they come as an embarrassment or a distraction, and we wish they would simply take a holiday and leave us alone.

The questions themselves surround such wide ranging and highly charged issues as ordination to church office, our images of God, sexual orientation and practice, and the fundamental nature of the church's mission in society and the world. We discuss the questions in small groups and major gatherings. We debate. We pray. The years roll by, and the questions remain. Whom shall we ordain to office, and whom shall we not ordain? How shall we, with finite language, speak of the infinite God? How shall we understand and respond to sexual orientation? In what ways do we, as the community of Jesus, relate to the political and economic systems of the world and of our country? The litany of questions continues, as does the awkwardness of our far from unified response to any one of them.

My thoughts on these questions are as passionate as those of any other person. I believe that our responses are vital for our witness in this present age. At the same time, I sense that beneath our struggles something immensely important is going on, and we will miss it if we focus only on the questions themselves. Indeed, the more I have experienced our communal handling of the tough questions, the more I sense that through all our wrestling and debate, we are being stretched at two critical points.

First, when we are at our best, the tough questions stretch us back to the roots of our faith experience. When I say "at our best," I mean those times when we pay attention to the primary stretching that comes with any form of conflict. I mean when we are prayerful, when we listen deeply, and when we speak respectfully to one another in Christ. If we allow this preliminary stretching to form us as a community, then we will be drawn to examine and know afresh the rich roots of our faith.

Examining our roots makes us scrutinize our own faith journey and discern what in that journey has influenced our thinking on the issue at hand. Doing this often demands that we wrestle with difficult passages of scripture. It causes us to listen again to the traditions and teachings of our particular community of faith.

Such examination of our roots can turn, of course, into little more than an exercise in partisanship. Some persons pull up their faith roots only to hit others over the head with them. When this happens, emotional appeals cloud important issues. Ears and minds snap shut on all fronts.

What I have increasingly seen, though, is an honest sharing of these roots. This happens wherever people take the time to search deeply and then find the courage to speak of what they have discovered. With conviction and true humility, they tell one another where they stand on the matter at hand and why. On most

occasions, no united opinion exists even at the conclusion of such sharing. No definitive path emerges no
matter how much persons may yearn for it. However,
what happens is perhaps more immediately needed. In
exploring and exposing roots, members begin to find a
commonness that lies deeper than any words, deeper
even than the divisions on the questions at hand.

One weekend I visited a large faith community that
had to vote on a highly divisive issue related to human
sexuality. Two members of the community in particular
shared from their roots. They did this with personal pain
and much vulnerability. One stood firmly on one side of
the issue. The other stood just as firmly on the other.
After the vote, the community fell quiet during the
counting of the ballots. With no prompting but that of
the Spirit, the two persons arose from their seats and
slowly walked toward each other. Before the vote was
ever announced, they embraced in our midst.

And it is in this place of vulnerability and sharing
that the second stretching takes place. Our attempts to
be Jesus' community, even in times of great tension,
draw us to see once again who we really are. For us, as
for the two who embraced while the ballots were being
counted, it is both a humbling and a freeing vision that
greets us. We come to see that we are human beings of
finite understanding who have somehow been called to
live out the desires of an infinitely loving God.

We do our best. We need grace all the way. Even
with our best efforts and God's grace, we still won't get
it completely right or see it whole. Life has been this
way ever since Abraham and Sarah. But if we seek in
faith, we will know the divine embrace that enables us

to embrace one another. Amid much brokenness around us and among us, this embrace is no small sign.

REFLECTION AND MEDITATION

1. Where have you been stretched for others in their need? Where have you been stretched by others whose faithfulness challenged your own?

2. Where has your community of faith been stretched for others? by others? Where do you sense stretching may be taking place right now?

3. How have you grown through involvement in a serious conflict?

4. What has helped you listen deeply to another or others in the midst of a conflict? As you listened, what did you learn about the other or others? about yourself?

5. What tough questions in the life of your faith community particularly stretch you? In what ways?

PRAYERFUL EXERCISES
To Grow in Awareness of Being Stretched
(personal with group adaptation)

1. After a time of coming to quiet, ask that you may see any occasions when you have been stretched because of your participation in the community of faith. Let these occasions come into your awareness.

2. Ask now in prayer that you may focus closely on

just one of these situations. In quietness, take time to enter it more fully. Sense once more how you were stretched. What did you feel? What aided you in the ways of growth? What do you still carry within you as a result of being stretched? You may wish to journal your responses. You may wish simply to be present to them within yourself.

3. Ask now that you may see any new stretching you are experiencing as a result of your participation in the community of faith. In quietness be present to this stretching.

4. Take time to picture the growth that may occur if you respond faithfully in this time of being stretched. Again, you may wish to journal what comes to you, or you may simply wish to be present in quietness to any image of growth you may receive.

5. Close with thanksgiving for all stretchings that have come to you in this time. Ask for continued awareness of all the ways in which life in Christian community calls you to grow.

If you are sharing this exercise in a group, go through movements 1–4 in quietness, with one person inviting the others to move from step to step. After movement 4, you may invite members of the group to share one incident where they have been stretched in the past and one place where they now feel they are being stretched. After the sharing, go to movement 5. In closing, it can be helpful to pray for one another's ongoing growth and for any particular needs for support that came forth during the sharing.

Prayer Practices in a Time of Conflict (*personal*)

In times of conflict, it can be helpful to adopt as a personal discipline any of the following prayer exercises.

1. *Cleansing prayer.* Take time daily to let any feelings of bitterness come forth, any hostilities, any deep anger toward others. Name these feelings or write them down. Ask that for today you be cleansed and set free of them as you respond to the conflict.

2. *Daily prayer for the other(s) with whom you are in conflict.* Draw into your mind those with whom you are in conflict right now. This may be hard but seek to picture them. You may be able to see their needs; you may not. Either way, quietly offer the persons into God's presence, just as you offer yourself. At the conclusion of this prayer time, give thanks for the grace of being able to offer the others; pray for God's steady working both in you and them.

3. *Prayer for awareness of the healing places.* Jesus' healing intent comes to life among us not just in the drama of full reconciliation. Given the depth of our brokenness, healing often begins to take shape in subtle ways: through a gentle growth in perspective and patience, through small gestures of understanding, through a growing sensitivity to one another's needs, perhaps through a greater peace in our own hearts about the whole situation.

   In this exercise, pray daily that you may grow alert to any ways that Jesus is bringing greater wholeness right now...within you...within the others...within the wider conflict. On those days when fresh insights come, give thanks for even the smallest of them; and pray that you continue to be open and responsive to any gifts of greater healing.

Prayer Practices in a Time of Conflict (*group*)

1. *Prayerful time with another.* If you are bearing the weight of conflict, it may help to find one other with whom you regularly lift in prayer any stresses you carry, any needs for perspective you feel, any bitterness from which you seek cleansing, or anxiety from which you seek release.

2. *Communal silence.* Before deciding on difficult issues, in the midst of heated discussion, or after a matter has formerly been resolved, it can be very helpful to invite the entire group into a time of quietness and prayer. Persons may wish to pray for wisdom, for attentiveness to the presence of the Spirit beneath all the deliberations, for awareness of the common needs of all.

3. *Communal petition for wholeness.* Let the one leading prayer acknowledge the existence of broken places. Simply let this one ask for openness: openness to the presence of the living Christ; openness to one another; openness to the small movements of healing, wherever they may come.

4. *Intercessory prayer group for wholeness.* Where there is extended conflict in the life of a faith community, a group may commit itself to the work of intercession for wholeness. The group may ask for prayer requests from any who wish to offer them.

On Tough Questions—Prayerfully Exploring Our Roots and Our Places of Growth (*group*)

This exercise is for use in any faith community that is experiencing substantial difference on an important issue. If the group is over twenty in number, form smaller groups made up of persons holding diverse opinions.

1. State the issue under consideration by the community simply, and indicate that the purpose of this time is to grow more aware of how God is working *with* all of us and *within* each of us as we struggle from our different perspectives. Then read Ephesians 4:1-6 and offer prayer for openness to the love God has for all and for openness to what each person will share.

2. Invite the participants to share their thoughts and feelings about the question at hand and also to state what experiences or teachings have brought them to their present understanding. Urge all to listen closely and respectfully to the words of the others.

3. Invite participants into a time of quiet reflection on where this issue most stretches them in their lives or where it is most painful. After a time of quiet and as they are led, participants may share how they are stretched or where they are in pain.

4. Close by reading Ephesians 4:1-6 again and proposing a time of open prayer of thanksgiving for any insights received, of petition for ongoing wisdom and continued growth, of intercession for one another's needs.

6

Formative Channels...

A S THE MONTHS of reflecting on Christian community passed, I increasingly became aware of certain channels through which the loving God shapes and renews our identity as a people. Initially these channels barely made it into my notes. They appeared along the edges of my weekly explorations or coursed through the background; other matters claimed primary attention. At length, their persistent presence demanded a regard that they had deserved all along.

Three of the channels bore no surprise when it came to naming them: the water of baptism, the body and blood of Christ, the word of scripture. The surprise came in seeing afresh how truly communal each of these channels is, and, alas, how much we have privatized their meaning. Three other channels emerged that I did not expect: vows, hallowed days and seasons, and hope of the Resurrection.

In a real sense, each of these channels is a beginning point. Each marks a place where the eyes of our spirits start to open. Each is a site of new seeing. From a purely logical standpoint, I might have treated them more fittingly at the start of the book rather than near its conclusion.

Yet when it comes to how we live in Christian community, my experience of these channels is more "in the midst" than "at the start." Our journey begins with baptism, but baptism informs our communal life along the way. The bright light of Resurrection may awaken us in the midst of our darkest and most personal grief, but it also kindles the vision that guides us daily as the community of Jesus' followers. The vows we utter in community are not private, nor is their import confined to the moment in which we speak them. They perpetually mold the life we share together.

This book's placement of these channels simply mirrors one facet of their work among us. They are foundational, but their full meaning as foundation emerges most clearly in the context of our ongoing life together. Through them God both sustains and shapes us in the midst of all that we do.

Of course, our formation through these channels requires choice as well as grace. As gifts of God the channels are ever available to our communities of faith. The question is whether we fully avail ourselves of them. Ignore them or entertain them with scant engagement of the mind and heart, and little will happen. We will remain closed to what they offer. If, however, we wait upon them prayerfully and expectantly, then they become vehicles for the rich nourishment of our common life.

In treating these channels, I feel it important at the outset to indicate that I am not trying to relate the helpful and sometimes complex doctrines that delineate their meaning. I am simply lifting them up for our awareness and reflection and attempting to evoke, in some small way, the blessings that each can impart to our common life.

WATER

In recent years I have found my eyes wandering toward the grandparents during the administration of the sacrament of baptism. I hope this modest deviation on my part doesn't count as irreverence. I am not at the point in my life where I find myself envying the grandparents. However, in one of the congregations to which I relate, the grandparents stood where I could not miss them, and something caught my eye. Perhaps I saw only a projection, a reflection of my own inner musing. But I think not. Something clearly moved across their faces. I'm not sure I can fully describe it, but I shall try.

As the parents and congregation responded to questions in the liturgy, the grandparents simply gazed. Not because they had nothing to say. They gazed because that seemed to be their vocation for the moment. And in all its intensity, their gaze spoke. Their eyes brightened as they admired their grandchild. Beyond anything else though, those same eyes firmly said, "There, now you belong! By the outpouring of water and the Holy Spirit you have become part of the many. You are claimed. You are surrounded. You are welcomed!"

In no way would I claim that the grandparents knew more about baptism than did the child's parents, but the whiteness of their hair and the weathered texture of their skin bespoke a sacred distance. Their lives had taken shape in years that would seem "long ago" to the child.

The child they looked on represented ties to a future they could but dimly imagine. And in the gaze of the grandparents lay the gratitude that eternally they and the child would be of one community. There lay the joy that the same living Christ and the same age-long company of companions who had nourished them would also nourish this child. There lay the knowledge that the same fellowship of Head and Body that had so stretched and blessed them would stretch and bless the child as well.

The grandparents gazed...and I watched, grateful for their gaze.

I have heard that in an ancient Coptic rite of baptism, persons to be baptized stand on one side of the baptismal pool while church members dressed in brilliant white robes stand on the other. Those receiving baptism enter the pool and go under its waters completely. As they emerge on the side of those in the church, they find themselves enveloped in white robes identical to those worn by the company awaiting them. They are more than cleansed. They are part of the new community.

I have seen an act less dramatic but just as rich in its proclamation. Immediately following the baptism of an infant, the pastor cradles the little one and walks back through the entire congregation repeating softly, "Meet Sarah (or James or Michelle), child of the covenant." This moment quietly reminds us that we and the child now are bound together in the most enduring of ways.

The water of baptism flows wide even as it washes deep. On the most personal and intimate of levels it is God's indelible mark upon my soul. Yet it is also the gentle stream that links me to others. And as I revisit baptism through the years, as I witness the simple rite again and again, I realize anew that the water pours forth continuously for us all. Enlivened, caught up in its current, we become a people who live together from the freshness of an ever-flowing love.

BODY AND BLOOD

She was nearly seventy years old and an ordained elder in her congregation. She was tall and lean and, at this moment, was dressed in a quilted red gown. She stood next to the young pastor who was holding bread for a long line of congregants who filed up the aisle to partake of the sacrament. They received the bread from him, took four steps to the side and stopped directly in front of her. She held the cup. "This is the blood of Christ, the cup of salvation," she repeated softly. She smiled at each of the persons receiving. Her smile was as natural as the sound of her voice and the slight nod of her head when she spoke the words.

After receiving the sacrament, I returned to my pew and, under the tutelage of her smile, became aware of the richness of life that filed toward the Communion table: people of all ages, some dark, some pale, strong and bent, tentative and bold. I saw the fiercely intense and the blissfully relaxed, those with eyes on the ground and those with eyes raised up and bright. Doubters and questioners and wonderers, biblical literalists, partisans of the political right, and passionate supporters of the left—on and on they came. She kept smiling. "This is the blood of Christ, the cup of salvation."

I could not see into the minds of those who moved past me, but whatever played within each one had at some time played within all of the others and within me. I sensed yearnings for mercy, for food to nourish the spirit, for assurance. I perceived desires for Christ's living presence, for quietness to meditate on his gift and receive it anew, and for an easing of pain. And perhaps above all, I keenly sensed a need to connect once again with the company of followers—followers physically present and followers already gathered into his perfect wholeness.

On and on they filed as they yearned, desired, sought. And she kept saying softly, "This is the blood of Christ, the cup of salvation." From the other end of the table came a younger voice, "This is the body of Christ, given for you."

Finally the last persons passed before the table. The minister and elder served each other. The entire congregation prayed. We sang a hymn, then bundled up and went out into the damp February air. A few walked along the city streets. Most got into cars and headed off.

Within minutes we parted, yet what we had received continued to bind us. We returned to places of pain and of laughter and of silence. Some of us journeyed into what we didn't know at all and others into what we knew only too well. And we were still of all ages... dark...pale. Strong and bent. Tentative. Bold. Doubters, questioners, and literalists. Passionate supporters of the political right and partisans of the political left. All of us now bore the gifts of the body and the blood.

And she with the smile and the quilted red gown had seen most clearly. The body and blood draw us to a oneness deeper than all our surface differences, deeper even than the differences that often appear to matter so much.

From where she stood she could comprehend what takes place every time we partake with a spirit of openness. At the table differences melt, and brokenness is overcome. Here we bring our aching needs and receive the truly elemental food—the body, the blood—given that we might become whole. As we partake of the body and the blood, we receive the One who receives us all and then sends us forth, a dazzlingly diverse company, to share his life-giving ways.

WORD

It is a sad and obvious fact the scriptural word periodically becomes a channel for division in the community of faith. On nearly every major ethical and theological issue, the same thing happens. At least it does in certain portions of the community. Proponents of one side line up their favorite passages while proponents of the other side haul out their own supporting passages. Or, in a development that confuses onlookers and participants alike, both sides employ the same passages but interpret them in opposite ways.

If we examine the use of the written word in our common life, other distressing matters come to mind. Some passages are obscure. Some offend contemporary tastes. The passages may be on target; but the offense remains, and nobody likes being offended. Some preaching on the Word is dull, trite, or just plain silly.

"Wouldn't it be better if we just set the Bible to one side and didn't bother with it any more?" grumbled one old fellow who prided himself on being a borderline heretic. He spoke with a slight twinkle in his eyes. The teenaged girl across from him caught the twinkle.

The straight-backed woman to his left missed it completely, pursed her lips, and said "Pffft." The teenager didn't say anything, but she smiled back at the older man. She sensed that he was on to something and that it had nothing at all to do with getting rid of the Bible.

And indeed, the Bible is not the issue in our common life. The issue revolves around our use of the Bible. Do we confine our reading of it to the familiar and the comfortable? Do we approach it to bolster some conclusion we have already reached? Or, following a different way, do we open ourselves to the Bible's challenges? Do we wait on it expectantly, knowing that however many times we have heard a passage it still has more to teach us? Are we willing to live with the uncertainty the written word can create for us as we struggle with its meaning?

"I find the Bible constantly drives me to question things," I heard an eighty-year-old minister say to a congregation that had invited him back for a special occasion. "It causes me to wonder about how I'm using my time and about how open I am to God in my daily routines. It forces me to wrestle with all sorts of things I still don't fully understand, like forgiveness and grace. And," he added, "it is the questions that have kept my faith alive and growing." This man was allowing the word of God to stir him up.

In our communities of faith, the Word becomes a channel of freshness and formation for our common life precisely when we allow the stirring to take place. The stirring can come in all forms and all moods. We listen to words of deep assurance:

God is our refuge and strength,
    a very present help in trouble.
Therefore we will not fear,
      though the earth should change,
    though the mountains shake
      in the heart of the sea;
though its waters roar and foam,
    though the mountains
      tremble with its tumult.
                    —Psalm 46:1-3

We hear these words. Do we then let ourselves, as community, live from the confidence they impart? Do we probe the words, and in the probing become increasingly one with the gift they share? What will it mean if we become a people who say from the depths, "We will not fear"? When we allow the Word to stir such wonderings among us, we begin to live in new ways.

Or the voice of a prophet catches us:

And what does the Lord require of you
but to do justice, and to love kindness,
    and to walk humbly with your God?
                —Micah 6:8

We listen; and in faithfulness to the Word, we begin the search. Where can we show the justice the Word clearly invites us to share? How shall we love kindness this coming week? this afternoon? in the next hour? How shall we, as a people, walk humbly with God in this tangled season of humankind's history?

"An unanswered question is a fine travelling companion. It sharpens your eye for the road," writes Rachel Naomi Remen.[1] If we receive the Word openly, it will give us questions and sharper eyes for the road.

The Word whips up our wondering. It expands our search. And if we let it stir us, then even where interpretations differ, even where we struggle to understand, we begin to center our common life not on ourselves but on the One who has beckoned to us through the Word from the beginning.

Vows

Vows echo softly through our life in community. Sometimes we share them in solemnity, sometimes in great joy. They come forth as we journey together through time. We profess or promise to follow a particular path as a result of our faith. We hear the question, "Will you …?" and leaning on God's grace we respond, "We will." Such speaking—now from one, now from another, sometimes from the whole body—offers a steady, voiced accompaniment to the life we share.

Some speak vows at the baptism of an infant. They will watch over the child and shape their lives so that the little one may, above all else, come to know the blessings of life in Christ. Some take vows of ordination or of bearing office in the church. Some pledge themselves to a specific task in society or to the discipline of intercessory prayer. In the context of community, persons exchange vows of marriage and vows of singleness. And all of these particular vows rest upon a common vow to follow in the way of Christ.

As I have witnessed the working out of vows in the life of Christian community, I have come to see three truths. First, in the simplest of analogies, vows are like hidden supports in a well built house. We don't run around saying, "Look at those trusses!" Nobody calling on friends in a new home ends the visit with, "I am particularly impressed with the two-by-fours you have behind your living room wall." Yet the inconspicuous, little noted support does much to hold the entire structure in place. Vows are just like this: much present, often beneath the surface, capable of upholding the order and even the beauty of what we share.

Second, if we would sustain the vows we make, then we must seek God's gracious aid. It is no coincidence that in Christian communities of all denominations, prayer accompanies the sharing of vows. When we vow, we pray. And we pray not just to hallow the vow. We pray, knowing that fulfillment of the vow lies beyond us. Only with the support of the all-loving, all-sustaining God shall we remain faithful to what we have just said.

And third, vows become a channel for blessing in our common life. When I began to reflect regularly on community, I noticed something I missed before. Where ties of community were strong, I repeatedly encountered persons trying to take seriously some promise they had made within their wider community of faith. Often my encounters were quiet. They occurred in places of struggle nearly as often as in places of joy. Yet just as neglect of vows brought hurt, I could see that attentiveness to them yielded goodness for the entire body. "Kind God, help me be faithful to this bond of love." "Grant me wisdom as I care for this child." "Help us find the courage to lead this community in the way we promised we would!" Such prayerful adherence to the good paths we have determined to follow can uplift the entire community.

HALLOWED DAYS AND SEASONS

For some years I served as pastor to six congregations spread through the green forests and rolling hills of western Pennsylvania. When my first Holy Week approached, all six congregations wanted a Good Friday service. My devoted predecessor had established this tradition, and clearly, the churches expected me to continue. Distance precluded a combined service. It came down to having four Good Friday services four nights in a row. That was how it had worked and how it would work.

I must confess that although I was somewhat experienced in pastoral ministry by this time, I was a bit squeamish. How did the people feel about this? After all, they were having to decide who would have the Good Friday service on Tuesday, who would have it on Wednesday, who would have it on Thursday, and who would actually get to observe Good Friday on Friday.

"Look," explained one relaxed and seasoned coal miner, "for us it's not the exact day that's so all fired important. It's what happens that matters." With that he nodded and said nothing more.

With no further discussion, everyone voted to continue the tradition. Through the next eight years and thirty-two Good Fridays, I never regretted it.

I have thought long on the wisdom of that miner's statement: "It's what happens that matters." In even the simplest of religious heritages, we set aside particular days and seasons. Naming them is easy: Advent, Christmas, Lent, Palm Sunday, Maundy Thursday, Good Friday, Easter. In my own denomination Epiphany and Pentecost have reclaimed attention since I became an adult. For many of our communities additional days and seasons extend the list: the Baptism of our Lord, Candlemas, Ascension Day, Ordinary Time, and Christ the King Sunday to name but a few.

And yet the naming of these hallowed times is secondary. "It is what happens that matters." In Advent we prepare. We look within, and we see our need. We pray for openness and cleansing that we may fully receive the One who comes. At Christmas God incarnate enters the heart of our struggle. On Ash Wednesday we bear our dust, and on Palm Sunday we celebrate deliverance. Holy Saturday reminds us again of how deep our waiting for deliverance must be. Through Easter, Pentecost, even Ordinary Time, the community pauses, opens, is acted upon, receives.

God's action upon us in such times is not abstract or fixed. It comes in the most solid and surprising ways. One Sunday in Advent I worshiped with a congregation in the southern portion of our presbytery. A construction job that was to have been wrapped up by election day had just gotten started. Scaffolding claimed the center of the sanctuary. Pews were shoved every which way. Nobody knew where to sit. The pastor, somewhat obscured by steel beams, announced, "When God is coming, God doesn't wait for perfection. In the midst of our whole mess, whatever form it takes, God comes!" That summed up the message for the morning. The next Sunday someone had put bows on the scaffolding.

In that same sanctuary not many months later, at the conclusion of a Good Friday service, the congregation filed out in silence. Suddenly there was a stirring by the doors that led out into the night. Voices whispered. People bunched together. My wife and I looked. In the midst of a growing cluster of people, we saw the face of a woman much loved by that body of persons. She was living with a virulent form of cancer, and many had not seen her in weeks. She had chosen this night to come back to be with them. Her firm embrace and her "God bless you" spoken from the heart marked us deeply.

"It's what happens that matters," said the miner.

And what is it that happens? What causes us to find meaning in an ill-timed construction project? What causes us to tie bows on scaffolding that blocks our view? Why does a woman bend every ounce of her carefully monitored strength to be with others on a night that honors Christ's death? And why does someone who does this move us so?

The miner wisely kept silent after his initial statement. None of us can put into words fully what "happens." It eludes definitive articulation. We will never nail it down completely.

And yet we receive hints of an answer. The miner knew them, and I sense that he knew them more fully than I. I suspect that the hints came for him in the same way they come for all of us: In hallowed days and seasons our time is touched and claimed by God's eternity. The redeeming reality that embraces us in the midst of our scattered and broken ways begins to shape us. In the words of theologian Jack Stotts, on entering the hallowed times and partaking of the sacred celebrations, "One recovers and places at the center of one's practice what is unique to one's identity."[2] And we begin to be shaped again, not by fad or by pressures around us or within us but by the One who says, "Lo, I am with you....I have overcome....Go forth as a new people in my name."

HOPE OF THE RESURRECTION

It happened weekly throughout my initial year of journaling on the places of community in Christ. Somewhere among the churches of our region, persons would gather because one among them had died. Basically the rhythm was and is the same every time. People come together to pray, to seek comfort in their grief, and to offer care for those closest to the one who has died. They give thanks for any goodness they have known and hear promises of fresh life. Sometimes they sing. Then quietly they go forth.

In the midst of the steady and somewhat distant rhythm of such services, a dear friend of mine died. I suddenly found myself in a very different place—a place where we all have been. The grief cut close and deep. My friend was old, had been in failing health; his death was expected. He was, though, as dear to me as family. He had coached me out of some exceptionally dumb behavior as a young pastor. The night my mother died, he had driven no small distance to pray with me and my wife. Though hundreds of miles now lay between us, we still kept in touch. When his daughter reached me at work with news of his death, I telephoned my wife and told her. As soon as the words came out of my mouth, neither one of us could speak.

I flew back to attend the service. I needed to be there. So did others. University folk. Advocates of the poor and the poor themselves. Middle-aged adults who had gone canoeing with our friend when they were teenagers. His children and grandchildren. His wife and his siblings. Colleagues who had the privilege of working with him far longer than I. Some of us knew each other well. Others of us knew only that we were drawn together by the same thankful memories and the same inner need.

And so in the most personal of ways, we came together in the sanctuary. We prayed. We sought comfort for our grief and comfort for those closest to our friend. We heartily gave thanks for his goodness and, doubting he needed any mercy, prayed for it anyway. We listened to promises of fresh life. We sang. Afterward we went to the fellowship hall and visited with one another, quietly at first. Then we began to tell stories of our friend, to laugh, to rejoice in all the goodness.

When it came time to go, we went out lifted in spirit. I know that in part this was due to the gathering itself. The sight of old friends had buoyed us. So too had the good memories. So too had the chance to reach in love toward his family and to one another.

Something else, I sense, had lifted us as well. It had touched us and invited us without making any demands. It had sounded in words we hear over and over again in such circumstances, words we shall never completely grasp, yet somehow they always beckon:

> We do not want you to be uninformed, brothers and sisters, about those who have died, so that you may not grieve as others do who have no hope (1 Thess. 4:13).

> "Do not let your hearts be troubled. Believe in God, believe also in me. In my Father's house there are many dwelling places. If it were not so, would I have told you that I go to prepare a place for you? And if I go and pre-

pare a place for you, I will come again and will take you to myself, so that where I am, there you may be also" (John 14:1-3).

In all these things we are more than conquerors through him who loved us. For I am convinced that neither death, nor life, nor angels, nor rulers, nor things present, nor things to come, nor powers, nor height, nor depth, nor anything else in all creation, will be able to separate us from the love of God in Christ Jesus our Lord (Rom. 8:37-39).

The words spoke a triumph we could not and cannot fully comprehend but a triumph nonetheless clear and unmistakable. Triumph for our good friend. And triumph not only for him, but for what he pointed us to so persistently: good sense, a passion for justice, work with the poor, a sense of fun, the capacity to forgive.

I flew home the next day realizing, as too seldom I do, that we truly are a community set free: free to grieve openly as we need to and must, free to express the losses we feel. But also free, even in the midst of loss and grief, to meet the hope that wells up from beyond us; free to keep in our hearts all the goodness we have cherished in another, knowing that even death will not take it away. We are free to act in our own lives and to act boldly, knowing that no shadow, no threat, not even death itself can ever separate us from the One we seek to serve.

REFLECTION AND MEDITATION

1. Where have you and your community of faith been shaped in your life together by any of these channels? In what ways?

2. Of the six channels explored in this chapter, which appears to be quietest in its operation in your community? Which appears to receive the greatest attention? Which is most neglected? In what way?

3. What can lead communities to neglect these channels or fail to see their communal importance? What can help us develop awareness of their formative presence once again?

4. What other channels has God given for the upbuilding of life in Christian community?

PRAYERFUL EXERCISES
Meditation on the Baptized Community
(*personal or group*)

If a group shares in this exercise, invite members to share openly at movement number 4.

1. Take time to reflect prayerfully on the event of your own baptism. Whether you were baptized as an infant or as an adult, visualize those who were near to you, who prayed for you, who welcomed this moment in your life. Take time to reflect on the commitments that you made or that were made out of love for you at the time of baptism.

2. In quietness picture or name to yourself bonds that have grown for you because of your baptism...paths you have followed...invitations you have experienced in your life.

3. Now let others in the baptized community come to mind: persons you have known, persons who have

shared your call in life even if you have not known them, persons from past eras in the life of the church, persons from eras yet to come.

4. Close with a time of thankfulness for all blessings that you have received through your baptism and for the gift of your baptism itself.

A Discipline of Awareness—Vows (*personal or group*)

The importance of vows in our common life is often understated or simply not recognized. To grow in awareness, make a commitment to pause once each week for six weeks and reflect on the questions:

- Where in recent days have I seen a person or persons live out some vow of faithfulness made within the context of the faith community? As you reflect on this question, consider the wide variety of vows made in community life: vows of marriage and singleness; vows of office bearing; vows of responsibility for tasks, for prayer, for the nurture of others.

- What blessings are growing for these persons because of their faithfulness? What blessings grow for the wider community?

If you are taking part in this exercise as a group discipline, meet every two weeks to share with one another what you have seen.

Meditation on a Neglected Channel (*personal or group*)

This exercise is for increasing awareness of and engagement with a neglected channel.

1. Either in a group or in personal mediation, ask to become aware of some channel of communal formation that your faith community currently neglects or

observes without engagement of mind and heart. If you are in a group, discern together the channel that will be the center of your reflection. If several channels arise for you, select one, holding any others for later consideration.

2. Take time to reflect on the causes of neglect. Visualize or write them down as they come to mind.

3. Turn your thoughts now to what the community life lacks because of its neglect of this channel. Prayerfully ask to see any vision that is lost, any bonds that weaken, or any other consequences that arise.

4. If you are in a group, share together any insights that have come in the quietness.

5. Close with a time of thanksgiving for any new understandings you have received, even those that are painful. Pray for a greater awareness of this particular channel and for sensitivity to ways that the community can grow fully open to its presence.

Meditation on the Richness of a Channel
(*personal or group*)

This exercise encourages us to sense more fully the richness that comes through any of the channels God offers for shaping and upbuilding our common life.

1. Begin by focusing on one particular channel: one of the six in this chapter or another channel you have seen. If you are sharing this exercise in a group, select one channel for your focus together.

2. Let come into your mind specific times when your community has drawn upon this channel. Be present to these times. Recall what happened in them.

3. Now let arise in your mind any goodness that has come through this channel...any specific blessings...any challenges...any new insights.

4. If you are taking part in this exercise as a group, share what has come to each member. If you are engaging in this exercise as a personal discipline, you may find it helpful at this point to journal any insights that have arisen for you.

5. Close with a time of giving thanks for the channel, for the rich number of ways it is present, for the blessings that come through it. Ask that you and your community may be formed continuously by its presence.

7

Ongoing Call...

BENEATH ALL our experiences of community in Christ there sounds an ongoing call. It bids softly. At times we may not hear it at all. The experience of community itself may have caught us and claimed our total attention. We now may be giving ourselves to the moments of coming together and their particulars. Often this is exactly what we need to do. We have no room in our lives for added hearing. At other times we simply may ignore the call and set it aside.

Yet whether we notice the call or not, whether we heed it or not, the call persists. It emanates from all those realms where God would stir up love among us. And on those occasions when we do hear it, we realize that what beckons us is nothing less than a persistent summons to enter still more deeply into community in Christ.

Some persons respond to this call with much activity. They buy books, attend studies, go on retreats. They enter discussions and make communal commitments. They openly state their intentions and seek to live more fully in community with others.

Others respond to the call by persevering in long-followed paths with their faith community. They too will discuss communal life with one another, review where they are, reach for greater wholeness. They will deepen well-worn tracks, watch out that these do not become ruts, and will remain open to fresh discoveries.

Still others follow a more silent way. They may not articulate what they are seeking to do even to themselves. Yet they prayerfully respond to an inner invitation to enter the common life more fully. They grow deep, both in their awareness of community and in the strength of the bonds they share with others.

In a sense, the call to deepen our community in Christ thrusts us back to the "Beginnings" cited at the start of this book. Having tasted the holy gift of community, we hunger for it all the more deeply. Having grown in our awareness of its presence, we seek to live even more fully into its richness. We may be further along in our life with community than when we started, but the ongoing call lets us know that whatever distance we have covered, we are still just beginning to learn the territory.

And ultimately the call points us to just this: the possibilities of an ever fuller immersion in Christian community. It does this in part by leading us to deal with the question that each community of faith must ask itself: Is Christ honored? It does this by opening us to wider beckonings where we catch hints of community forming beyond our usual expectations of where it lies. And in our current historical context particularly, the ongoing call leads us to sense the Spirit inviting us to give ourselves yet further to the gift of community as it is fashioned and led forth by the Living Christ.

IS CHRIST HONORED?

I have never heard the question so earnestly put. It happened during my denomination's General Assembly, a massive annual affair that lasts seven days and is at once draining, trying, aggravating, and immensely uplifting. When I came down for breakfast the second day, I noticed a sign in the hotel lobby that read, "Meditation Room—23rd Floor." After an exceptionally intense morning I found myself in the elevator pushing button number 23.

When I got off on the appointed floor, I heard something of a racket coming from behind a door sporting a yellow "Meditation" sign. The year before a similar room had been silent. The noise, however, was no greater than what I had just left, so I figured I might as well go in. Upon opening the door, I found myself staring at fifteen people jammed into a tiny room. They were praying out loud and, well, in a fashion that I am not exactly used to.

One of the persons looked up, smiled broadly, and motioned me to join them. Already off balance, I lurched around the long legs of the man who several days later would ask the question. Two people on the rug scooted apart. I landed between them. The prayers continued.

After twenty minutes the leader of the group said, "All right, let's just pause for a bit." He welcomed me, as did the others. They asked their questions gently. Who was I? What was I about at the Assembly? Feeling somewhat awkward, I gave my name, my official "observer" status, and my present state of residency. Their greetings continued. "Good to have you!" "We're glad you came up here." The leader explained that they were part of a prayer vigil for the Assembly. They had begun their work the day before it convened and would continue through its adjournment. I was welcome to join them at any time. Having said this, the man drew the group back into prayer. I stayed with them another half hour, then quietly left. A couple of them smiled at me as I went out the door.

After this unexpected encounter, I found myself returning to the group daily. Sometimes they prayed in total silence. Other days they prayed as resoundingly as when I first met them. One morning a woman in the group was caught up in anguished prayer for the entire denomination. She wept as she prayed. Members of the group felt deeply about certain issues before the Assembly, but their prayers were void of the let's-pray-for-our-side spirit one might have anticipated. They simply sought wholeness and faithfulness in their wider community of faith. Throughout this time, their hospitality and warm welcomes continued.

The last afternoon I saw them, I learned that the long-legged fellow had just come off an eight-day fast for the Assembly. He made absolutely nothing of this. It came out through one of the prayers. We discussed his fast briefly during a period of group sharing. At this same time I mentioned that in the morning I had attended a large worship service for the Assembly commissioners. Hearing this, the man looked directly at me and asked with deep feeling, "Was Christ honored?"

I hesitated in my response—not because I doubted the answer. I simply needed to take in the fullness of his question. Only then could I reply on the same level. At length I offered a single word: "Yes."

"Then God be praised," the man said, leaning back and closing his eyes.

On my way down in the elevator thoughts began that have been with me ever since. The Assembly itself had gone forth with much work on the part of many people. Debate at points had been painful, feelings strong, the hours nearly interminable. Persons on the Assembly floor and in committee rooms had shared moments of joy, understanding, reconciliation. And here, across the street from the meeting place and twenty-three stories up, a small group of persons had prayed without ceasing, travailed, fasted, rejoiced, warmly welcomed, and cared. I knew, as did they, that some might mock their fervency, but that really did not matter. What mattered was that they had offered the much needed gift of intercessory prayer, and they had done this for a single purpose. They had yielded themselves so that, through all the passion and turmoil of their broader community of faith, Christ might be honored.

The man's question touches on every element of our life together. It reaches into the heart of our largest faith communities and our smallest. In handling conflict, do we honor or dishonor the One we claim to serve? Do we indulge the blocks to our common life, or do we name them and bend every effort to set them aside? Do we rejoice at being stretched for others in their need or at the very least seek the grace that this may happen? Or does our common life turn inward and constrict the horizons of our concern?

Our honest speech with one another, our simple acts of being present, and our words of encouragement all honor Christ. So does our faithfulness in keeping vows, in receiving the sacraments of grace, in letting the Word shape our journey. And when we neglect the elemental practices, when we treat lightly the channels through which we are nourished as a people, then we separate ourselves from the One who would make us a whole and vital people. The question "Is Christ honored?" hovers about all the occasions where, season to season, we gather in Christ's name.

In essence, the question draws us back to the basics of our allegiance. In our common life do we seek to honor Christ?...self?...our own desires?...our small group of people? Where do we root ourselves? Toward what do we aim? We know the right answers to all these questions. We may state them easily enough. The living of the answers can be another matter.

When we do dare to live the answers, we come to a place of grace and growth. I suspect the man who fasted eight days and asked the question knew this in ways that I will spend a long time learning. He forthrightly pressed a matter that too often I keep at the back of my mind. I can imagine that is where a lot of us keep it. And yet the question remains, and it points us to the center of all we do. Shall we honor the One who gives us the gift of our life together? Each time we prayerfully try, we venture further into the wholeness God has invited us to know.

WIDER BECKONINGS

The call to enter further into community in Christ emanates not only from the center of our experiences with Christian community. It also beckons from wider and unexpected directions. Friends have pressed me on this matter in helpful ways. While I was in the midst of my first year of journaling about Christian community, one friend asked, "Are all the true communities you see explicitly Christian?"

My spiritual director raised the issue in a slightly different form: "Be aware, Steve, not only of the Christian community of which you are a part. Try to see any other genuine communities that intersect with your life, even if they do this only briefly." This was a spacious invitation. My director did not define what she meant by *genuine*. She did not even indicate whether the term *Christian* should overtly be attached to these other groupings. She simply encouraged me to stay open.

The question from my friend and the words of my director touched on a reality I was encountering with some frequency. I was meeting community in places where, even if Christ was not declared, something Christ-centered was being born. By this I am not referring to moments of shallow comradeship. I don't mean clubby gatherings or those incidents of hail-fellow-well-met congeniality that surface around unimportant issues. What I was encountering was of a wholly different order.

The day after the bombing of the Murrah Federal Building in Oklahoma City, I found myself in a massive traffic jam on Interstate 94 between Battle Creek and Kalamazoo. I land in one of these messes about four times a year. The experience is always the same. Cars stretch out of sight. Horns honk. A few people try to cruise the shoulder and butt in. You can see faces mouthing the words "Oh, my gosh!" and stronger.

On this particular day, nothing of the sort went on.

We sat still in sweltering heat, inched forward, then sat still some more. We worked the clogged highway together as a single, somber body: truckers and drivers of compacts, full-sized cars, jalopies. A few people sat in vehicles that for most of us would claim better than a year's salary. From time to time we glanced at one another, nodded encouragement, signaled an opening if it looked like someone needed to change lanes. On a solemn Thursday afternoon, an event that touched the lives of thousands drew us into one.

On a crystalline night two months later, I brought out a telescope that spends too much time in our basement. Our neighbor's children came over. We scanned bright cliffs and dark craters on the moon. As the night turned cooler, we shifted to the Milky Way as it flows through Cygnus and then, with a move of the scope that forever stuns me, we found ourselves staring at the Great Star Cluster in Hercules: a perfect globe, a million stars radiating into the near nothingness of space. We "Aaaahed." And we fell silent. And we stood together until we all knew it was time to go.

What do we encounter in such moments? What can we name it? We surely are not "in church." For the most part the label "Christian community" does not enter our minds. In the traffic jam on I-94 we weren't saying, "It's un-Christian to honk and butt in line at a time like this; therefore we will not do it." And yet the immensity of communal sorrow gripped and shaped us as a body. That body briefly resembled the community that calls us to learn and live the lessons of compassion for one another in our need.

Beneath the starlit sky, the neighbor's children and I

did not burst into old songs from church camp. We set up no markers that proclaimed, "God is with us in this place." Yet we were unmistakably grasped and shaped. Our quiet closeness bore kinship to the closeness that takes hold of us in times of formal, corporate communion with the living God. I'm not talking about nature worship here. I'm talking about the experience of being drawn together in deep and undeniable ways.

What happens in such times? What meets us in such experiences of quiet and overwhelming power? We may not speak the answer, but inwardly we know. An ancient chant sings it over and over again:

> *Ubi charitas et amour*
> *Deus ibi est.*
>
> Wherever there is charity and love
> There is God.

If love flows among us, even briefly, God is there—in traffic jams, in places of staggering beauty, in the realms of darkest communal pain. If we find ourselves bound together even momentarily, God is present. We taste with our spirits the community God longs to build.

To honor these occasions of community is to acknowledge how widely and all inclusively God works to fashion bonds among us. It is to open ourselves in wonder to the One who beckons toward wholeness at every turn. I believe this is what my friend with his question and my director with her counsel were trying to help me see.

And yet by honoring these experiences, we do not hold them up as substitutes for formal religious communities that gather in Christ's name. Only in the long-term bonds of such community will we learn where all these matters point. The formal community itself stands as a sign of what our passing experiences of closeness suggest. And rather than distracting us, these experiences of wider beckoning may ultimately be a means by which the living God calls us to fuller immersion in the community of faith that is both our home and our place of ongoing growth.

SPIRIT INVITING

One morning I met with a small group of leaders who bore wide-ranging responsibilities in their community of faith. These eight people were intimately linked with every phase of their community's life: its care network, its financial maintenance, its education, its outreach to new lives, its worship life, its attentiveness to needs on its doorstep and faraway. I asked them a single question: "How would you characterize your life together?"

The oldest member of the group, a woman with several decades of history in its membership, gave her answer: "We've been rediscovering what God can do among us." After a slight pause, a young man seated next to her added, "We're rediscovering; and at this point, I don't think we can stop."

These words came not as a boast but as a description. Nothing more, really. And certainly nothing less. I found it instructive that the eldest and youngest members of the group shared the response. They possessed an obvious unity on the matter, as did the others seated around the table.

For a time we probed the two halves of their answer. What did they mean by "rediscovering what God can do among us"? Their responses here were down-to-earth, undramatic, deeply felt. The group members were, one said, "actually talking about God again." They were growing more open in their prayer life. As leaders, they had been fostering a spirit of mutual encouragement throughout the wider body. In times of conflict and on tough issues, they sought to guide the community with greater openness, honesty of speech, and deeper listening. The community as a whole was giving renewed attentiveness to the quality of its worship life and to those places where it was being stretched for others in their need. None of this had happened overnight, nor had any particular direction reached its fulfillment. Still these leaders and their community were rediscovering new levels of life together in Christ.

"And at this point, I don't think we can stop." Why? What attracted the group members? What kept drawing them on? The answer here proved more elusive. First responses included, "We're finding too much just to stay where we are" and "There always seems to be more for us to explore." Experientially these were wholly valid answers even if they didn't quite give the full picture. Finally one answer seemed to embrace the other answers and tie them to their root: "We can't stop because the Spirit keeps inviting us further."

I believe that last response describes the experience of many contemporary communities of faith. The Spirit is inviting, inviting us to overcome our shyness and to discover anew what community in Christ is really meant to be. The Spirit is inviting us to set aside our idealized images of community, because true community in Christ involves us in all the realities of human relationships.

The Spirit is inviting us to attend once again on faithful practices and on being stretched and on our steady, prayerful need for grace in the life we share together. In essence, the Spirit now bids us to enter a form of being and acting that has no limits. It is calling us to grow in our life with the community that is both fashioned and led forth by the Living Christ.

This invitation comes in the context of much need. "We must live in community because God wants us to respond to the unclear longings of our time with a clear answer of faith," wrote Eberhard Arnold in the 1920s.[1] The words are still pertinent today. I am convinced that our quiet, steady, imperfect efforts to grow in community will do far more for the renewal of the church of Jesus Christ and for the world Christ came to redeem than will all our anxious critique and all of our perpetual efforts at bureaucratic reorganization. The steady living of love's way is desperately needed. It is this that will speak faith's message to the unclear longings of our time.

The invitation to enter further into Christian community comes as fresh forms of common life are emerging and as old forms take on new life. A small group meets regularly for prayer and mutual support. A congregation previously limited by narrow vision begins to explore its neighborhood, its prayer life, and the ways its members can talk honestly with one another. A retreat center starts playing host not just to individuals but to groups that come seeking to grow closer in the life they share. Such seemingly small beginnings take place about us almost ceaselessly.

The small beginnings, while easily overlooked, are

vital. We cannot say what form Christian community will take 100 years from now. Much is changing for our parishes and congregations, for religious orders and for all our institutional expressions of community. But wherever we now respond to the Spirit's invitation, wherever we care faithfully for what is emerging among us, there we are letting Christ form us for the goodness of community that will be.

The invitation to give ourselves further to the gift of community in Christ is, ultimately, a persistent summons to become one with the mystery of God's healing work. Where we honor Christ in our communities of faith, we take part in that work. Where we open ourselves to the wider beckonings of God's movement in the world around us, we sense the all-embracing vastness of this mystery. And where in small, steady ways we give ourselves to the growth of community in Christ, we let ourselves become both pattern and sign of God's ceaseless yearning, known both among us and around us

> as a plan for the fullness of time,
> > to gather up all things in him,
> > > things in heaven and things on earth.
> > > > —Ephesians 1:10

✹

REFLECTION AND MEDITATION

1. Where in the past have you sensed the Spirit's invitation to enter more deeply into community in Christ? Where might you be sensing that invitation now?

2. Where do you believe your faith community has learned to honor Christ? Where has it failed or been weak in doing so? In what particular ways is it being called to honor Christ now?

3. Think of your community experiences outside your faith community. What have they been, and what are they like? What did you learn from them?

4. Where have you seen fresh forms of community in Christ? older forms being deepened?

5. What clear, needed gifts can community in Christ offer to the unclear longings of our time?

PRAYERFUL EXERCISES
To Grow in Awareness of the Ongoing Call
(*personal or group*)

If used in a group, let a leader direct each of the steps, and the entire group share at movement 3.

1. After a time of quiet, ask that you may become aware of any places where you are called to deeper participation in the life of community in Christ. Write or hold in your mind any particular thought that comes.

2. In quietness now simply be present to the call that you sense. Let its reality grow for you. Reflect on its particulars: How does it come? What does it ask of you? What grace will you need in order to respond?

3. If you are following this as a personal exercise, journal any additional insights that have come to you.

If you are taking part in the exercise as part of a group, share with one another what has arisen for you and consider prayerfully:

- What are the implications for all of us in what we are hearing?
- How can we support one another in responding to the ongoing call?

4. Close with a time of thanksgiving for any fresh awareness of call that has come, petition to continue to grow in awareness, and prayer to follow steadily in the way of God's beckoning.

A Group Examen—"Honoring Christ"

1. Begin with a time of quiet prayer for openness to the leading of God's spirit.

2. Consider in silence, "Where have we known the grace of honoring Christ in our common life?" After a period of quiet, let members share any places where they sense honor is being given.

3. Again in silence, ask to see any places where Christ is neglected or dishonored in the group's life. Let members share with one another any places or concerns that have come to mind.

4. Close with a time of thanksgiving for the gift of any places where Christ is honored and prayer for grace to grow in honoring him in any places of weakness or neglect.

Wider Beckonings—Reflection and Prayer *(group)*

1. Let each person prayerfully consider, "Where have I experienced community, even momentarily, outside the customary channels of my faith community?"

Allow these situations to come into awareness. Then let one of them come to particular focus.

2. Continuing in quietness, let each consider the specifics of the one situation that has drawn to focus: What was the experience like? How did it strike you or move you at the time…and later? What in particular did you learn through this experience?

3. Let persons now simply share what has come to them in the time of reflection.

4. Close with thanksgiving for one another's experiences and for all the ways that God is at work to draw persons into unity.

Meditation on the Union of All Things in Christ Jesus
(*individual or group*)

1. After a time of quietness, let Ephesians 1:3-10 be read slowly by one person if a group is sharing in this exercise.

2. After further quietness, read verses 9 and 10 again:

   He has made known to us the mystery of his will, according to his good pleasure that he set forth in Christ, as a plan for the fullness of time, to gather up all things in him, things in heaven and things on earth.

3. In quietness let come into mind:
   - all realms of human experience, large and small, where oneness in Christ is growing; take time to reflect on these, to name them inwardly, to see their blessings, to give thanks for them;
   - all realms of human experience where there is still separation; take time to reflect on these, to sense any movement or yearning toward unity, to pic-

ture the goodness of unity arising in the midst of brokenness;

- your own community of faith; take time to picture or name any ways that your community currently is sharing in the upbuilding of the unity of all things in Christ.

4. Enter into a time of spoken or silent prayer of

- thanksgiving for all the places where unity grows;
- intercession for places where unity is needed;
- petition that your faith community may take part in building up the ways of unity and peace.

5. Close by reading once more Ephesians 1:9-10.

Epilogue:
Late-Night Reflections...

I AM NO longer sure of the genesis of the words that follow. They arose one night; I jotted them down hastily and then stuffed them into a file from which they fell unceremoniously while I was working on the preceding pages. I cannot say precisely what churned in my mind as I wrote them. The particulars of that night have long vanished. The words do seem to have emerged from that place where the personal journey is stretched by the call to be in journey with others. As I look over these words now, I find them incomplete. Such words always are. And yet they tug at me, and I am grateful for the tugging....

Christian Community is where my pride is punctured and where I come to see the wonderful gifts of others. It is where I am repeatedly called to be patient with others and then to see that others are called to be patient with me.

Christian Community is where my own stage in life meets the stages of so many others both older and younger than I, and it is where I at last can pause in my business and see the stunning beauty of all the stages of life God has made.

Christian Community is, at its foundation, where I learn what it means to have Christ at the center—not that I place him there myself. Rather he reasserts himself through the fresh waters of baptism, through the bread and the wine, through Word that speaks deeply to my needs and to the needs of others who, like me, have come to the One who can make us whole.

In Christian Community I learn that I am not alone in my need for mercy, and again in Christian community my own vision of love is expanded constantly by those whose vision is different from mine but just as real and often broader.

And in Christian Community, as repeatedly I am called to tasks I cannot do myself, here, with others who also lean on the Living Christ, I learn that not of ourselves but of the Spirit we can do what lies at hand. We can carry forth on the healing way.

Notes...

CHAPTER 1

1. Douglas John Hall, "Theology and Worship Paper No. 5," *An Awkward Church* (Louisville, Ky.: Presbyterian Church USA, 1993), 24.

2. Barry Lopez, "Homecoming" in *Field Notes*, (New York: Alfred A. Knopf, 1994), 103ff.

3. Dietrich Bonhoeffer, *Life Together* (New York: Harper & Row, 1954), 29–30.

CHAPTER 2

1. Paul S. Minear, "Idea of Church," *The Interpreter's Dictionary of the Bible*, vol. 1 (New York: Abingdon Press, 1962), 617.

2. Edward C. Sellner, *Tales of the Celtic Saints*, audiocassette tape (Notre Dame, Ind.: Ave Maria Press, 1993).

CHAPTER 3

1. Douglas V. Steere, "Intercession: Caring for Souls," *Weavings: A Journal of the Christian Spiritual Life* 4, no. 2 (March/April 1989): 17.

2. Barbara Fiand, *Where Two or Three Are Gathered* (New York: Crossroad Publishing Co., 1992), 91.

CHAPTER 4

1. John S. Mogabgab, "Editor's Introduction," *Weavings: A Journal of the Christian Spiritual Life* 8, no. 2 (March/April 1993): 2.

CHAPTER 5

1. "The Theological Declaration of Barmen," *The Constitution of the Presbyterian Church USA: Part 1: The Book of Confessions* (Louisville, Ky.: The Office of the General Assembly, 1983), paragraph 8.17.

2. Mehdi Dibaj, quoted in *The 1995 Mission Yearbook for Prayer & Study* (Louisville, Ky.: Mission Interpretation and Promotion, Presbyterian Church USA, 1995), 161.

3. *So Full of Deep Joy: Songs by the Monks of Weston Priory.* Weston Priory Recording Co. Audio recording.

CHAPTER 6

1. Rachel Naomi Remen, *Kitchen Table Wisdom: Stories That Heal* (New York: Riverhead Books, 1996), 293.

2. Jack Stotts, *Beyond Beginnings: Occasional Paper No. 2* (Louisville, Ky.: Theology and Worship Ministry, Presbyterian Church USA, 1989), 12.

CHAPTER 7

1. Eberhard Arnold, *Why We Live in Community*, trans. of *Warum wir in Gemeinschaft leben* (Farmington, Penn.: Plough Publishing House, 1995), 7. Original essay published in *Die Wegwarte*, October/November 1925.

Suggested Reading. . .

Ackerman, John. *Spiritual Awakening: A Guide to Spiritual Life in Congregations*. Washington, D.C. Alban Institute, 1994. This helpful resource integrates individual spiritual needs with corporate spirituality.

Arnold, Eberhard. *Why We Live in Community*. Foreword by Basil Pennington and two interpretive talks by Thomas Merton. Farmington, Penn.: Plough Publishing House, 1995. A brief and beautiful statement of the nature of Christian community originally written in the 1920s; the interpretive talks by Merton, given in 1968, and the Foreword by Pennington, written in 1995, highlight the ongoing themes and challenges of community as they play from decade to decade in a predominantly secular world.

Benedict of Nursia. *The Rule of St. Benedict*. Translated and with introduction and notes by Anthony C. Meisel and M. L. del Mastro. Garden City, N.Y.: Doubleday & Company, 1975. The excellent introductory material and notes highlight the major themes of this classic statement of Christian community in its monastic form.

Bonhoeffer, Dietrich. *Life Together*. Translated and with introduction by John W. Doberstein. New York: Harper & Row, 1954. Written for students of an underground seminary of the German Confessing Church during the height of Nazi powers, this small volume offers a beautiful exploration of the disciplines and rhythms of being apart and being together in Christian community.

Buchanan, John M. *Being Church, Becoming Community*. Louisville, Ky.: Westminster John Knox Press, 1996. Wonderfully written, this book presents the underlying Biblical and theological understandings of community as they are lived out in the worship and activities of a congregation. It also explores the responsibility faith communities bear in relation to the human needs surrounding them.

Fiand, Barbara. *Where Two or Three Are Gathered*. New York: Crossroad Publishing, 1992. This is a thoughtful and sensitive probing of religious community life in a time of cultural change. Though written primarily for men and women in religious orders, it contains many helpful insights for persons in parishes and small group communities.

Olsen, Charles M. *Transforming Church Boards: Into Communities of Spiritual Leaders*. Washington, D.C.: Alban Institute, 1995. The fruit of much careful work with church boards and the leaders of congregations, this book contains immensely helpful suggestions for letting church boards once again become places of spiritual formation and sources of vital spiritual leadership.

Stotts, Jack. Papers delivered to various governing bodies of the Presbyterian Church USA: "Beyond Beginnings" (1989) and "Friendship in the Church?" (1993), reprinted and available from the Congregational Ministries Division, Presbyterian Church USA, 100 Witherspoon Street, Louisville, Ky. 40202-1396. Written with great care and obvious devotion, each paper explores the current context in which the Christian community finds itself and the biblical models that can inform our understanding and guide our ongoing movement toward communal faithfulness.

About the Author...

STEPHEN V. DOUGHTY, an ordained minister of the Presbyterian Church (USA), is Executive Presbyter for the seventy-one congregations of Lake Michigan Presbytery. Prior to his present call, he spent twenty-three years serving as pastor to congregations in northern Appalachia, the Black Hills, and the St. Lawrence River Valley. A writer and retreat leader, Doughty holds a certificate in spiritual formation from the Shalem Institute, where he studied with Tilden Edwards and Gerald May. He also has earned degrees from Williams College and Yale University. He and his wife, Jean, live in Kalamazoo, Michigan.